101
BBQ AND GRILL
RECIPES

PAGE 44
GRILLED SKIRT STEAK
with smoked butter

101
BBQ AND GRILL
RECIPES

MOUTHWATERING WAYS TO FLAME-GRILL, SMOKE, AND SIZZLE

COMPILED BY
Dan Vaux-Nobes

DOG 'n' BONE

First published in the United Kingdom
in 2015 by Ryland Peters & Small
20–21 Jockey's Fields   341 E 116th St
London WC1R 4BW   New York, NY 10029

www.rylandpeters.com

10 9 8 7 6 5 4 3 2 1

Recipe text © Valerie Aikman-Smith, Fiona Beckett,
Ghillie Bhasan, Vatcharin Bhumichitr, Dr Burnorium,
Heather Cameron, Maxine Clarke, Clare Ferguson, Felipe
Fuentes Cruz and Ben Fordham, Dan May, Jane Noraika,
Elsa Petersen-Schepelern, Louise Pickford, Linda Tubby,
Lindy Wildsmith, and Ryland, Peters & Small 2015

Recipe introduction text © Dan Vaux-Nobes

Design and photography © Dog 'n' Bone Books 2015

A CIP catalog record for this book is available from the
Library of Congress and the British Library.

ISBN: 978 1 909313 54 5

Printed in China

Editor: Rosie Lewis
Designer: Eoghan O'Brien

Picture credits: see p144

CONTENTS

INTRODUCTION

IS THERE ANY FORM OF COOKING MORE REAL AND PRIMAL THAN BARBECUING HUGE, BLOODY LUMPS OF ANIMAL CARCASS OVER A PIT OF RED-HOT GLOWING COALS? SWEATING, PRODDING, AND FLIPPING WHILE ENVELOPED IN ALL THAT HEAT AND SUN-PIERCED-SLOWLY-DRIFTING-CLOUDS OF SWEET-SMELLING SMOKE, WORKING AWAY LIKE A BLAST-FURNACE OPERATIVE AT THE SHARP END, DELIVERING PLATES OF BEAUTIFULLY SMOKY AND CHARGRILLED GRUB TO WILLING HANDS, WHILE SWIGGING ON YOUR PREFERRED ICE-COLD BEVERAGE.

As well as all that, it's often such a social thing. A real shared dining experience. An improbable mix of moms, dads, aunties, uncles, badly behaved children, and drunken buddies cooking, chatting, joking, and eating together. A dining event and an easy-going sense of occasion that many of us seem to have lost in our busy everyday lives—AND you get to cook and eat outside, or al fresco as they say in exotic foreign climes. In fact, if you squint your eyes and waft smoke from the grill into them till they're good and streaming, you could definitely be in Tuscany or something. Alright, that bit is total rubbish, your backyard is never going to be mistaken for the Tuscan countryside, but you get my drift.

There really is nothing quite like a barbecue. But you can ALWAYS do it better, and that's where this book comes in. A pack of frozen burgers and a bag of lurid pink sausages have their place (I suggest the trash), but you're much better than that, and you know it. So get reading the following recipes, drag the grill out of the shed, and have a stab at cooking some whole fish or a massive lump of meat so you can realize your true grilling potential.

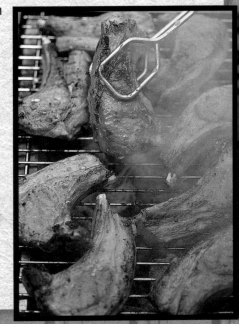

GRILLING GUIDELINES

CHOOSING A GRILL

Outdoor grills come in all shapes, sizes, varieties, and prices—from the small disposable aluminum ones sold in supermarkets or hardware stores, to larger and often hugely expensive covered grills. Some have both a grill rack and a flat plate, for versatility, but this is not essential. The recipes will work on any of the following.

Purists would probably argue that charcoal has to fuel a grill, but many people prefer (and find it easier to opt for) gas or electric ones. It is certainly debatable as to what will give the best flavor to the food, but it really comes down to personal choice.

For a charcoal grill, you can use either standard briquettes or hardwood lump charcoal. The former may contain chemicals from the process used to make them, which—although totally safe—may affect the flavor of the food. Hardwood lump charcoal is not as readily available as briquettes, but contains no additives, burns easily, gets far hotter, and lasts longer.

Portable grills are essential if you want to cook away from home (unless your chosen site has permanent grills), and these too come in a wide selection of styles. Be aware of weight, since someone has to carry it—the lighter the better. Portable grills can also be either charcoal- or gas-fired, but remember that coals stay hot for some time, so you must find somewhere you can legally and safely leave them or wait until they are completely cool before packing them in a bag to take away with you.

Safety is extremely important in grilling, especially if you are in parkland, as many places will be at risk from fire. Be sensible and set the grill up away from dry timber or grass. Always take a fire blanket or, if possible, a small portable fire extinguisher with you.

COOKING ON A CHARCOAL GRILL

Arrange the fuel in as large an area as your grill will allow, at least 4 inches (10 cm) deep and leaving a little room around the edges. Place a few firelighters among the coals and light them using a taper or matches—they will help to get the fire started. Once the coals are burning, leave the grill for 40–45 minutes, until all the flames have subsided and the coals are covered in gray ash. Hold your hand about 5 inches (12 cm) above the fire and count how long it can stay there. It will be only a couple seconds for a hot fire; 3–4 seconds for medium hot; and 5–6 seconds for a cool fire.

You can also determine the temperature for cooking by adjusting the height of the grill rack over the coals. Most charcoal grills have several rungs to set the wire rack on, the closest to the heat being the hottest and the farthest away the coolest. Cleaning is best done after you have finished cooking but while the grill is still assembled, so that any residual bits of food stuck to the rack can be brushed off into the fire. Do not clean the grill rack with soap or water, just scrub it well with a wire brush (see equipment, right).

GAS OR ELECTRIC?

Gas and electric grills can be adjusted in the same way as a domestic stove, by turning the temperature up or down. They often come with a hood, enabling you to cover the food as it grills, which produces a similar effect to roasting. Alternatively, leave the lid off and grill as normal.

It is important to preheat a gas or electric grill until it is really hot before adding the food, and then reduce the heat as necessary. This enables the food to brown quickly on the outside, sealing in the flavor, in the same way as on a more traditional charcoal grill.

Cleaning is also done in the same way as for the charcoal grill, although you can buy special cleaners from hardware stores. For best results, follow the instructions on the back of individual products.

EQUIPMENT

Long-handled tongs are essential for turning over food without allowing your hands to get too close to the heat and scorching. Do not leave the tongs on or near the heat, as they too can get very hot, resulting in burns.

Skewers can be either bamboo or metal. Bamboo skewers are disposable and will need to be soaked before use, to prevent them from burning over a high heat. Metal skewers are readily available from hardware stores, but remember they can get very hot, so turn them using a dish towel or tongs.

A sturdy wire brush is the best tool for cleaning and removing bits of stuck-on food from the surface of the grill or flat plate. Give the grill a good scrub all over after you have finished cooking, and rub the flat plate with a little oil to season it each time.

FOOD PREPARATION AND SAFETY

Get all the preparation done in advance—the day, the morning, or an hour or two before you eat. Marinating times in the recipes are flexible, so do what suits you. Salsas, relishes, dressings, and salads can be made in advance, but green salads should be dressed at the last minute. Once prepared, cover the food and refrigerate or store it in a cool place until you are ready to cook or serve it.

Most of the foods cooked on the grill will have started off raw. Although they must be stored in the refrigerator, it is best to return them to room temperature for about an hour before cooking. Always keep food covered with plastic wrap (clingfilm) or a clean dish towel while it is waiting to be cooked, to keep off the bugs. Once it has reached room temperature, food should be cooked as quickly as possible to prevent it from spoiling.

Once the coals are ready, arrange the meat on the grill and give it time to brown before turning. Once the meat has browned, turn it frequently and move it around the grill to ensure even cooking. You may need to raise the grill height if food is cooking too fast, or lower it so that it is nearer the coals if it is too slow. To lower the heat, dampen the coals slightly or close the air vent.

Make sure you cook chicken, burgers, and pork thoroughly. They should be piping hot all the way through, none of the meat should be pink, and the juices should run clear. Cut into meat to make sure it is cooked thoroughly. One of the major causes of food poisoning is cross-contamination, so it is essential to keep raw and cooked food apart. When transferring cooked meat, fish, or poultry from the grill, make sure to use clean utensils and place them on a clean cutting board or platter, not back in the unwashed dish you used to transport them to the grill.

HAVE A STAB AT COOKING SOME FISH OR MEAT AND START REALIZING YOUR TRUE BBQ POTENTIAL.

CHAPTER 1
HERE'S THE RUB

THROUGHOUT THE RECIPES IN THIS BOOK, YOU'LL BE ASKED TO MARINATE STUFF, ESPECIALLY MEAT. WHAT YOU'RE DOING IS BASICALLY SOAKING THE OBJECT YOU'RE MARINATING IN FLAVORED, SEASONED (AND MORE LIKELY THAN NOT, ACIDIC) LIQUID (THE MARINADE), BEFORE COOKING IT. THE REASON YOU'RE GOING TO ALL THIS TROUBLE IS TO ADD LOVELY FLAVOR AND, IN THE CASE OF MEAT, TO TENDERIZE IT. HERE ARE THREE CRACKING MARINADE RECIPES. ALTHOUGH THEY ARE MULTIPURPOSE, I RECKON THE HERB, LEMON, AND GARLIC WOULD BE PARTICULARLY GOOD WITH STEAK, THE MINTED YOGURT WOULD WORK WELL WITH LAMB, AND THE THAI SPICE WITH CHICKEN. BUT FEEL FREE TO SLING ANYTHING AND EVERYTHING INTO THESE MARINADES AND SEE WHAT HAPPENS.

MARINADES

THAI SPICE MARINADE

* Using a sharp knife, trim the lemongrass stalks to 6 inches (15 cm), then remove and discard the tough outer layers. Chop the inner stalk coarsely.

* Pound the lemongrass stalks, lime leaves, garlic, ginger, cilantro (coriander) roots, and chiles in a mortar and pestle to release the aromas.

* Put the mixture into a bowl, add the oils and fish sauce, and set aside to infuse until ready to use.

2 lemongrass stalks

6 kaffir lime leaves

2 garlic cloves, coarsely chopped

1-inch (2.5-cm) piece fresh ginger, peeled and coarsely chopped

4 cilantro (coriander) roots, washed and dried

2 small fresh red chile peppers, seeded and coarsely chopped

1 cup (200 ml) extra virgin olive oil

2 tablespoons sesame oil

2 tablespoons Thai fish sauce

makes about ½ pint (300 ml)

2 teaspoons coriander seeds

1 teaspoon cumin seeds

1 cup (250 ml) thick yogurt

freshly squeezed juice of
½ lemon

1 tablespoon extra virgin
olive oil

2 garlic cloves, crushed

1 teaspoon grated fresh ginger

½ teaspoon sea salt

2 tablespoons chopped fresh mint

¼ teaspoon chili powder

**makes nearly ½ pint (about
275 ml)**

MINTED YOGURT MARINADE

* Put the spices into a dry skillet or frying pan and toast over medium heat until golden and aromatic. Remove from the heat and let cool. Transfer to a spice grinder (or clean coffee grinder) and crush to a coarse powder. Alternatively, use a mortar and pestle.

* Put the spices into a bowl, add the yogurt, lemon juice, olive oil, garlic, ginger, salt, mint, and chili powder and mix well. Set aside to infuse until ready to use.

HERB, LEMON,
AND GARLIC MARINADE

* Strip the rosemary and thyme leaves from the stalks and put into a mortar. Add the lemon zest, bay leaves, and garlic and pound with a pestle to release the aromas.

* Put the mixture into a bowl and add the crushed peppercorns and olive oil. Set aside to infuse until ready to use.

2 sprigs of fresh rosemary

2 sprigs of fresh thyme

pared zest of 1 unwaxed
lemon

4 bay leaves

2 garlic cloves, coarsely
chopped

1 teaspoon black
peppercorns, coarsely
crushed

1 cup (200 ml) extra virgin
olive oil

makes about ½ pint (300 ml)

RUBS ★

SLAPPING A RUB ONTO WHATEVER MEAT OR FISH YOU'RE COOKING ADDS FLAVOR IN A VERY SIMPLE AND DIRECT WAY. YEAH, IT'S MESSY, AND IF YOU'RE ANYTHING LIKE ME, NO DOUBT YOU'LL GET COVERED IN IT, BUT THAT'S HALF THE FUN. IF THERE'S SUGAR IN THE RUB, IT'LL CARAMELIZE AS IT COOKS. IF YOU WANT STRONGER FLAVORS, SLAP MORE ON, OR, APRÈS SLAP, WRAP YOUR MEAT, FISH, WHATEVER, IN PLASTIC WRAP (CLINGFILM) AND LEAVE IT IN THE FRIDGE FOR A COUPLE OF HOURS TO LET THE RUB GO TO WORK AND BE PROPERLY ABSORBED. BUT, OF COURSE, IF YOU'RE IMPATIENT OR HUNGRY, THESE WILL WORK FINE STRAIGHT AWAY. HERE ARE THREE RUB RECIPES TO BE GETTING ON WITH. THEY'LL WORK ON ANYTHING, REALLY, BUT TO ME, THE CREOLE SAYS PORK OR BEEF, THE MOROCCAN LAMB, AND THE ASIAN RUB FISH OR CHICKEN. THEY MIGHT SAY SOMETHING DIFFERENT TO YOU, THOUGH, SO FEEL FREE TO IGNORE ME AND DO WHAT FEELS RIGHT.

MOROCCAN RUB

1 tablespoon coriander seeds

1 teaspoon cumin seeds

2 cinnamon sticks

1 teaspoon whole allspice berries

6 cloves

a pinch of saffron threads

1 teaspoon ground turmeric

2 teaspoons dried onion flakes

½ teaspoon paprika

1 teaspoon sea salt

makes about 6 tablespoons

* Put the whole spices and saffron threads into a dry skillet or frying pan and toast over medium heat for about 1–2 minutes or until golden and aromatic. Let cool then transfer to a spice grinder (or clean coffee grinder) and crush to a coarse powder. Alternatively, use a mortar and pestle.

* Put the spices into a bowl, add the remaining ingredients, and mix well. Set aside to infuse until ready to use.

CREOLE RUB

½ small onion, finely chopped

1 garlic clove, finely chopped

1 tablespoon chopped fresh thyme

1 tablespoon paprika

1 teaspoon ground cumin

¼ teaspoon cayenne pepper

1 tablespoon brown sugar

1 teaspoon sea salt

a little freshly ground black pepper

makes about 6 tablespoons

* Put all the ingredients into a small bowl, stir well, and set aside to infuse until ready to use.

ASIAN RUB

4 whole star anise

2 teaspoons Szechuan peppercorns

1 teaspoon fennel seeds

2 small pieces of cassia bark or 1 cinnamon stick, broken

6 cloves

2 garlic cloves, finely chopped

grated zest of 2 unwaxed limes

1 teaspoon sea salt

makes about 6 tablespoons

* Put the whole spices into a dry skillet or frying pan and toast over medium heat for 1–2 minutes or until golden and aromatic. Remove from the heat and let cool. Transfer to a spice grinder (or clean coffee grinder) and crush to a coarse powder. Alternatively, use a mortar and pestle.

* Put the spices into a bowl, add the garlic, lime zest, and salt and mix well. Set aside to infuse until ready to use.

SALSAS

I HAD NO IDEA THAT SALSA IS SPANISH FOR "SAUCE," BUT NOW I'VE PONDERED IT FOR HOURS, IT MAKES TOTAL SENSE. ANYWAY, WHEN WE TALK ABOUT SALSA WE'RE ALL NO DOUBT THINKING ABOUT MEXICAN CUISINE. IT SEEMS THEY HAVE THE MARKET CORNERED WHEN IT COMES TO THESE TYPES OF SAUCE. SALSAS GO WELL WITH PRETTY MUCH ANY BARBECUED FISH OR MEAT, ARE SUPER-EASY TO MAKE, AND ADD A MUCH-NEEDED BIT OF CITRUS AND VEGETABLE ACTION TO WHAT WILL NO DOUBT BE A COMPLETE MEAT-FEST. THERE'S A WHOLE BUNCH OF RECIPES TO TRY. MY PARTICULAR FAVORITES ARE SALSA VERDE WITH STEAK (BUT IT'S ALSO REALLY GOOD WITH FISH), SALSA BRAVA— "WILD SAUCE"—BECAUSE IT'S SCORCHIO AND I LOVE A BIT OF HEAT. I ALSO LIKE THE FACT THAT SALSA BRAVA IS WHAT YOU GET ON TOP OF PATATAS BRAVAS IN SPAIN, SO YEAH, IT'S GOOD WITH POTATOES. FINALLY, YOU'VE GOT TO HAVE A GO AT MAKING GUACAMOLE, ESPECIALLY IF YOU'VE ONLY EVER TRIED NASTY SUPERMARKET VERSIONS, BLITZED TO A FINE, BLAND PASTE. NO! THINK CHUNKY AND FULL OF FLAVOR. YEAH!

CORN AND PEPPER SALSA

2 large corn cobs

3 tablespoons sunflower oil

4 scallions (spring onions), trimmed and thinly sliced

freshly squeezed juice of 1 lime

6 Pepperdew bell peppers, finely chopped

2 tablespoons finely chopped fresh cilantro (coriander) leaves

a dash of chili sauce or a large pinch of chili powder (optional)

sea salt and freshly ground black pepper

serves 4

* Holding the corn cobs upright, cut down the sides with a sharp knife to remove the kernels. Heat a large skillet or frying pan over medium heat and add 2 teaspoons of the oil. Stir-fry the corn for 2–3 minutes, until it begins to brown. Add the scallions (spring onions) and stir-fry for 1 minute. Transfer to a bowl and let cool for 10 minutes.

* Add the lime juice, peppers, cilantro (coriander), and the remaining oil and mix well. Add a dash of chili sauce, if using, and season.

TOMATO SALSA

1 lb. (500 g) ripe tomatoes, skinned and finely diced

½ red onion, finely chopped

1–2 small green chile peppers, seeded and finely chopped

3 tablespoons freshly squeezed lime juice

a pinch of superfine (caster) sugar

2 tablespoons finely chopped fresh cilantro (coriander)

sea salt

serves 4

* Put the tomatoes in a large bowl with the onion and chiles. Add the lime juice and mix well, then add the sugar and season with salt. When ready to serve, add the cilantro (coriander).

SALSA VERDE

4 rounded tablespoons finely chopped fresh flat leaf parsley

1 rounded tablespoon finely chopped fresh mint leaves

2 rounded tablespoons finely chopped fresh basil leaves

scant ½ cup (100 ml) extra virgin olive oil

3 scallions (spring onions), trimmed and finely chopped

2 garlic cloves, very finely chopped

2 tablespoons capers, rinsed and finely chopped

2 tablespoons gherkins, rinsed and finely chopped

3 anchovy fillets, finely chopped

2 teaspoons Dijon mustard mixed with 2 tablespoons red wine vinegar

freshly ground black pepper

serves 4–6

* Put the herbs in a bowl with half the olive oil. Stir, add the scallions (spring onions), garlic, capers, gherkins, and anchovy fillets and mix well. Add the mustard and vinegar mixture, then add enough of the remaining olive oil to make the salsa slightly sloppy. Season to taste with freshly ground black pepper.

SALSA BRAVA

----

4 tomatoes

3 Habaneros or Scotch Bonnet chile peppers, stalks removed

½ onion, roughly chopped

4 garlic cloves, peeled

2 tablespoons vegetable oil

4 tablespoons crushed dried chilis

sea salt

makes a bowlful

★ Heat the oil in a pan for 1 minute. Remove from the heat, add the crushed chilis and stir well.

★ With a pestle and mortar, crush the roasted chilis, onion, and garlic very well for about 3 minutes.

★ Add the chili oil and crush again for 3 minutes.

★ Add the roasted tomatoes and pound well for another 2 minutes, then mix in ⅔ cup (175 ml) water and a couple of pinches of salt. Continue to pound until all the ingredients are very well blended.

★ Preheat the oven to 350°F (180°C).

★ Put the tomatoes, whole chiles, onion, and garlic in a roasting pan and roast in the preheated oven for about 15–20 minutes or until evenly blackened, turning occasionally with metal tongs. Remove from the oven and allow to cool for 10 minutes.

AVOCADO SALSA

1–2 fresh green chile peppers, stalks removed

2 garlic cloves, peeled

6–8 fresh tomatillos, husks removed

3 tablespoons chopped fresh cilantro (coriander)

1 big tablespoon very finely chopped onion

2 ripe avocados, pitted and peeled

a pinch of sea salt

makes a bowlful

* Preheat the oven to 400°F (200°C).

* Put the chiles, garlic, and tomatillos on a baking sheet and roast in the preheated oven for 15–20 minutes, or until slightly charred.

* Cut the chiles in half and scrape out the seeds (or leave them in if you want to take it up a notch!). Put in a food processor with all the other ingredients and whizz for 2 minutes. Add a little water or salt, if required.

GUACAMOLE

2–3 avocados

1 medium bunch of fresh cilantro (coriander)

1 tomato

a pinch of sea salt

a pinch of ground white pepper

makes a bowlful

* Pit and peel the avocados.

* Scoop the flesh out into a bowl. Finely chop the cilantro (coriander) and add to the bowl with the salt and pepper. Roughly mash with a fork.

* Finely chop the tomatoes and stir into the guacamole.

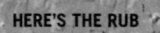

FLAVORED BUTTERS

I RECKON THERE ISN'T ANYTHING IN EXISTENCE THAT CAN'T BE IMPROVED BY THE ADDITION OF BUTTER. NO MATTER HOW GOOD YOUR BEAUTIFULLY COOKED PIECE OF MEAT, FISH, OR EVEN VEGETABLES, SLAP ON SOME BUTTER TO MELT. YEAH! INSTANTLY BETTER. ADD FRESH HERBS AND OTHER AROMATIC FLAVORS TO YOUR BUTTER AND YOU RATCHET IT UP EVEN FARTHER. IT'S RIDICULOUSLY EASY TO MAKE FLAVORED BUTTER (IN FACT, IT'S EASY TO MAKE YOUR OWN BUTTER—HONESTLY, LOOK INTO IT—BUT IF YOU'RE STARTING OUT, USE STORE-BOUGHT BUTTER AND EXPERIMENT AWAY). AS I MENTION ELSEWHERE, TRUST ME THAT ANCHOVY-FLAVORED BUTTER DOES NOT GO WITH CORN. HERE ARE THREE RECIPES TO GET YOU STARTED; ALL OF THEM WILL GO WELL WITH PRETTY MUCH ANYTHING.

CAPER BUTTER

2 tablespoons capers in brine,
drained and patted dry

1 stick (125 g) unsalted butter,
softened

1 tablespoon chopped fresh
flat leaf parsley

1 teaspoon finely grated lemon
zest

freshly ground black pepper

serves 4–6

* Finely chop the capers and put
in a bowl with the butter, parsley,
lemon zest, and pepper. Beat
together with a fork until evenly
combined.

* Transfer the butter to a small
piece of waxed (greaseproof)
paper and roll into a log. Wrap
the paper around the butter and
twist the ends to seal. Refrigerate
or freeze until required. Serve cut
into slices.

SAFFRON BUTTER

----

a large pinch of saffron threads

1 stick (125 g) unsalted butter,
softened

sea salt and freshly ground
black pepper

serves 4–6

* Soak the saffron in 1 teaspoon
of boiling water for 10 minutes,
then beat into the butter and
season. Transfer to a small
piece of waxed (greaseproof)
paper and continue to follow
the recipe for Caper Butter.

HERB BUTTER

2 tablespoons chopped fresh herbs
such as basil, chives, dill, mint,
or parsley

1 stick (125 g) unsalted butter,
softened

sea salt and freshly ground
black pepper

serves 4–6

* Beat the herbs and seasoning
into the butter until evenly
combined. Transfer to a small
piece of waxed (greaseproof)
paper and continue to follow the
recipe for Caper Butter.

SAUCES

ANY BARBECUED MEAT IS ALMOST ALWAYS INFINITELY BETTER WITH SAUCE DRIZZLED OVER THE TOP OR ON THE SIDE FOR DIPPING ACTION. THERE ARE SOME AMAZING READY-MADE SAUCES OUT THERE, BUT IT'S ALWAYS GOOD TO MAKE YOUR OWN, SO HERE ARE SOME RECIPES TO TRY. LET'S TALK ABOUT BARBECUE SAUCE FIRST: IT'S A CLASSIC AND GOES WITH MOST MEAT, ESPECIALLY PORK; NOT SO WELL WITH FISH. SWEET CHILE SAUCE ISN'T AS GOOD WITH CHARGRILLED MEAT AS BARBECUE SAUCE IS, BUT IT'S GREAT WITH CHICKEN, FISH, AND (ODDLY) CORN. ASIAN BARBECUE SAUCE IS PERFECT FOR GRILLED MEAT. BELL PEPPER BUTTER SAUCE SOUNDS DELICIOUS AS A DIP ON ITS OWN, BUT I'M THINKING LAMB. PIRI-PIRI IS GREAT WITH CHICKEN, BUT IT'S ALSO GOOD WITH SHRIMP (PRAWNS). SMOKY BARBECUE SAUCE IS AMAZING IN BURGERS AS WELL AS WITH BEEF, LAMB, AND CHICKEN.

BARBECUE SAUCE

1 cup (175 g) crushed tomatoes

½ cup (175 ml) maple syrup

2 tablespoons light molasses

2 tablespoons tomato ketchup

2 tablespoons white wine vinegar

3 tablespoons Worcestershire sauce

1 tablespoon Dijon mustard

1 teaspoon garlic powder

¼ teaspoon hot paprika

sea salt and freshly ground black pepper

makes about 2 cups (450 ml)

★ Put all the ingredients into a small pan, bring to a boil, and simmer gently for 10–15 minutes until reduced slightly and thickened. Season to taste with salt and pepper and let cool.

★ Pour into an airtight container and store in the refrigerator for up to 2 weeks.

ASIAN BARBECUE SAUCE

scant ½ cup (100 ml) tomato purée or passata

2 fl. oz. (50 ml) hoisin sauce

1 teaspoon hot chili sauce

2 garlic cloves, crushed

2 tablespoons sweet soy sauce

1 tablespoon rice wine vinegar

1 teaspoon ground coriander

½ teaspoon ground cinnamon

¼ teaspoon Chinese five-spice powder

makes about 1½ cups (350 ml)

★ Put all the ingredients into a small pan, add 3½ fl. oz. (100 ml) water, bring to a boil, and simmer gently for 10 minutes. Remove from the heat and let cool.

★ Pour into an airtight container and store in the refrigerator for up to 2 weeks.

SWEET CHILE SAUCE

6 large fresh red chile peppers, seeded and chopped

4 garlic cloves, chopped

1 teaspoon grated fresh ginger

1 teaspoon sea salt

scant ½ cup (100 ml) rice wine vinegar

½ cup (100 g) sugar

makes about 1 cup (200 ml)

★ Put the chiles, garlic, ginger, and salt into a food processor and blend to a coarse paste. Transfer to a pan, add the vinegar and sugar, bring to a boil, and simmer gently, part-covered, until the mixture becomes a thin syrup. Remove from the heat and let cool.

★ Pour into an airtight container and store in the refrigerator for up to 2 weeks.

BELL PEPPER BUTTER SAUCE

1 large red bell pepper

5 tablespoons unsalted butter, diced

1 tablespoon freshly squeezed lime juice

a pinch of saffron threads

a pinch of cayenne pepper

sea salt and freshly ground black pepper

serves 4

* Broil (grill) the bell pepper for 8–10 minutes, or until tender and charred all over. Seal in a plastic bag and leave until cool enough to handle.

* Skin and seed the bell pepper, chop the flesh, and put in a pan with the butter, lime juice, saffron, and cayenne. Heat through until the butter has melted.

* Using a food processor or hand blender, process the bell pepper mixture until smooth. Season to taste and heat through. Serve hot.

PIRI-PIRI SAUCE

8 red bird's eye chile peppers

1¼ cups (300 ml) extra virgin olive oil

1 tablespoon white wine vinegar

a pinch of sea salt

makes about 1¼ cups (300 ml)

* Finely chop the chiles (including the seeds), put in a bowl, and add the olive oil, vinegar, and sea salt.

* Transfer to a sterilized bottle and store in a cool place for up to 1 week.

SMOKY BARBECUE SAUCE

¾ cup (200 ml) tomato purée or passata

$1/_3$ cup (100 ml) maple syrup

3 tablespoons dark molasses (black treacle)

3 tablespoons tomato ketchup

3 tablespoons malt vinegar

3 tablespoons Worcestershire sauce

1 tablespoon Dijon mustard

1 teaspoon garlic powder

a pinch of Spanish smoked paprika

sea salt and freshly ground black pepper

makes about 1⅔ cups (400 ml)

* Put all the ingredients in a small pan, bring to a boil, and simmer gently for 10–15 minutes, or until reduced slightly, and thickened. Season to taste.

* Pour into a sterilized bottle and refrigerate for up to 2 weeks.

SMOKY CHILI BBQ SAUCE

THERE ARE SOME CRACKING BARBECUE SAUCES AVAILABLE, BUT ANY PROPER ALPHA-BARBECUE DUDE OR DUDETTE WHO'S SERIOUS ABOUT STUFFING THEMSELVES WITH "ALL THE MEAT" IS KNOCKING UP THEIR OWN. IMAGINE THE WELL-DESERVED SMUG LOOK ON YOUR FACE WHEN SOMEONE COMPLIMENTS THE SAUCE AND YOU IMMODESTLY ROAR "HELL YEAH" AS YOU ADMIT TO MAKING IT ALL BY YOURSELF. THIS RECIPE IS A PRETTY GOOD STARTING POINT. THE SECRET IS THE ADDITION OF CHIPOTLE AND JALAPEÑO CHILE PEPPERS TO MAKE IT EXTRA SCORCHIO. FEEL FREE TO ADAPT THE FLAVORS TO SUIT YOURSELF.

1 cup (240 ml) molasses

1 cup (240 ml) tomato ketchup

1 cup (240 ml) maple syrup

2 chipotle chile peppers in adobo sauce

2 jalapeño chile peppers, roughly chopped

2 scallions (spring onions), roughly chopped

2 roasted red bell peppers

1 yellow onion, roughly chopped

4 garlic cloves, peeled and crushed

a 3-inch (7-cm) piece fresh ginger, peeled and roughly chopped

freshly squeezed juice of 1 lemon

a large bunch of fresh cilantro (coriander), roughly chopped

sea salt and coarsely ground black pepper

makes 2½ cups (600 ml)

* Put all the ingredients in a blender or food processor and process until you have a smooth sauce.

* Store the marinade in an airtight container in the fridge for up to 2 weeks.

* To use, put the meat in a ceramic dish, pour the sauce over, and leave to marinate for 8–24 hours in the fridge. Let the meat come to room temperature, then cook as preferred. This sauce also works well with beef and poultry.

HOGWILD BOURBON GLAZE

½ cup (120 ml) bourbon
(such as Wild Turkey)

2 tablespoons molasses

1 tablespoon honey

½ teaspoon chipotle chili powder

2 garlic cloves, peeled and
roughly chopped

2 tablespoons chunky orange
marmalade

2 tablespoons olive oil

1 sprig fresh rosemary

sea salt and freshly ground black
pepper

makes 1 cup (240 ml)

★ Put all the ingredients in a
blender or food processor and
process until puréed and smooth.

★ Store the glaze in an airtight
container in the fridge for up to
2 weeks.

★ Marinate bacon, chops, ribs, and
pork roasts in the glaze overnight,
then remove from the glaze and
cook as preferred. Simmer the
remaining glaze for 10 minutes to
reduce, then serve on the side of
the cooked meat.

ADDING HARD LIQUOR MAKES MOST THINGS TASTE BETTER. THAT'S THE THINKING BEHIND THIS RECIPE, AND I CAN'T FAULT THE LOGIC. WHAT WE USE HERE IS THE SOFT TOFFEE FLAVOR OF BOURBON. SLAP IT ON! WHEN YOU'VE HAD A FEW YOURSELF, BE SURE TO WAX LYRICAL TO ANYONE CLOSE BY ABOUT THE SHARED TERROIR OF HOG AND THE GRAIN IN THE BOURBON, LEADING TO A HEAVEN-SENT FLAVOR MATCH. IT'S A LOAD OF GARBAGE, BUT IT NEVER HURTS TO BRING A LITTLE PRETENTIOUSNESS TO THE PARTY.

TO COOK A GREAT LUMP OF PORK, MAKE SURE YOU LAVISH SOME ATTENTION ON IT BEFORE SLINGING IT OVER THE COALS. "HOW?" YOU ASK. "RUN IT A HOT BATH? FEED IT BELGIAN CHOCOLATES? SETTLE DOWN ON THE SOFA WITH ITS FAVORITE TV BOX SET?" NO! ALL THESE IDEAS ARE VERY STUPID—IT'S A LUMP OF DEAD PIG. WHAT YOU REALLY WANT TO DO IS GIVE IT A RUB ALL OVER WITH THIS PIG SPICE MIX. MAKE IT SENSUAL, OF COURSE. WHEN YOU'VE FINISHED AND YOU'RE BOTH HAPPY, GRILL AND EAT ITS TASTY ASS.

HOG HEAVEN SPICE MIX

2 tablespoons dried sage

1 tablespoon dried thyme

1 teaspoon dried lemon
peel

1 teaspoon dried garlic
powder

1 teaspoon coarse sea salt

1 teaspoon ground white
pepper

makes 4½ tablespoons

★ Put all the ingredients in a bowl
and mix together.

★ Store the spice mix in a glass jar
with a tight-fitting lid for up to
6 months.

★ To use, rub the spices over
pork and cook as preferred.
Alternatively, add 1 tablespoon
of the spice mix to ½ cup
(120 ml) olive oil and use as
a dip for crusty bread.

CHAPTER 2

PARTY STARTERS

MOO PING PORK

1 teaspoon coriander seeds

4 garlic cloves, finely chopped

6 cilantro (coriander) roots, finely chopped

4 tablespoons Thai fish sauce

2 tablespoons light soy sauce

1 cup (250 ml) thick coconut cream

2 tablespoons groundnut (peanut) or safflower oil

1 tablespoon sugar

½ teaspoon freshly ground white pepper

1 lb. (500 g) lean pork, thinly sliced into pieces about 3 x 2 inches (4 x 7.5 cm)

lettuce, parsley, or cilantro (coriander), to serve

sauce

2 tablespoons Thai fish sauce

2 tablespoons lemon or lime juice

1 tablespoon light soy sauce

1 teaspoon chili powder

1 tablespoon sugar

1 tablespoon coarsely chopped fresh cilantro (coriander)

serves 4–12

TRADITIONAL THAI STREET FOOD, THE UNLIKELY SOUNDING MOO PING IS PERFECT BARBECUE FODDER. IT MANAGES TO TICK MULTIPLE BOXES, BEING SUITABLY EXOTIC, QUICK TO COOK, AND, MOST IMPORTANTLY, DELICIOUS. ALL THE REAL WORK IS IN THE PREP, SO GET THAT DONE AND THEN SIT BACK WITH A SINGHA BEER OR THREE BEFORE FIRING THE SKEWERS FOR A FEW MINUTES A SIDE, PREFERABLY ON THE BARBECUE FOR THAT AUTHENTIC SMOKY TASTE (ALTHOUGH A BROILER/GRILL OR STOVE-TOP GRIDDLE PAN WILL DO THE JOB TOO). PERFECT SERVED WITH STICKY RICE.

* Using a mortar and pestle, pound the coriander seeds, garlic, and cilantro (coriander) roots together in turn to form a paste. Then mix in the fish sauce, soy sauce, coconut cream, oil, sugar, and pepper until thoroughly blended. Add the pork and stir well, making sure each piece is thoroughly coated. Let stand for at least 30 minutes, but longer if possible.

* To make the sauce, while the meat is marinating, put the fish sauce, lemon juice, soy sauce, chili powder, sugar, and cilantro (coriander) in a small bowl and mix well. Taste—if too hot, add more fish sauce, lemon juice, and sugar.

* Preheat a grill/barbecue. Thread 2 pieces of meat onto each skewer, making sure that as much of the surface of the meat as possible will be exposed to the heat. (Make more skewers if you have meat left over.) Grill at a high heat for 2–3 minutes on each side, or until the meat is thoroughly cooked through. Serve on a platter with lettuce, parsley, or cilantro, with the sauce on the side.

PORK KOFTA KEBABS
with sweet and sour sauce

MEATBALLS ON A STICK! YOU CAN'T BEAT IT. NOT ONLY ARE THESE ASIAN-FLAVOURED MEATY BALLS DELICIOUS, BUT ALSO YOU'RE NOT LEFT CHASING THEM AROUND THE PLATE FRUSTRATINGLY WITH A FORK, OH NO. THESE BAD BOYS ARE GOING NOWHERE EXCEPT YOUR GOB, PINNED IN PLACE WITH A SKEWER FOR YOUR EATING PLEASURE. OH YEAH! SERVE THEM WITH NOODLES AND THE HOT DIPPING SAUCE.

2 teaspoons peanut or sesame oil

4 shallots, finely chopped

2 garlic cloves, finely chopped

1 lb. (500 g) ground (minced) pork

2 tablespoons Thai fish sauce

2 teaspoons Chinese five-spice powder

2 teaspoons sugar

2 handfuls of fresh white or brown bread crumbs

sea salt and freshly ground black pepper

noodles, to serve

sweet and sour sauce

2 teaspoons peanut oil

1 garlic clove, finely chopped

1 fresh red chile pepper, seeded and finely chopped

2 tablespoons roasted peanuts, finely chopped

1 tablespoon Thai fish sauce

2 tablespoons rice wine vinegar

2 tablespoons hoisin sauce

4 tablespoons coconut milk

1–2 teaspoons sugar, to taste

a pinch of sea salt

serves 4

★ To make the sauce, heat the oil in a small wok or heavy-based skillet or frying pan. Stir in the garlic and chile and, when they begin to color, add the peanuts. Stir for a few minutes until the natural oil from the peanuts begins to weep. Add all the remaining ingredients (except the sugar and salt) along with ½ cup (120 ml) water. Let the mixture bubble up for 1 minute. Adjust the sweetness and seasoning to taste with sugar and some salt, and set aside.

★ To make the meatballs, heat the oil in a wok or a heavy-based skillet or frying pan. Add the shallots and garlic—when they begin to brown, turn off the heat and leave to cool. Put the pork into a bowl, tip in the stir-fried shallot and garlic, fish sauce, five-spice powder, and sugar, and season with a little salt and lots of pepper. Using your hands, knead the mixture so it is well combined. Cover and chill in the refrigerator for 2–3 hours. Knead the mixture again then tip in the bread crumbs. Knead well to bind. Divide the mixture into roughly 20 portions and roll into balls. Thread them onto pre-soaked wooden skewers. Preheat the grill/barbecue and cook the kebabs for 3–4 minutes on each side, turning them from time to time, until browned.

★ Reheat the sauce. Serve the kofta with noodles and the hot sweet and sour sauce on the side for dipping.

SKEWERED SCALLOPS
with coconut dressing

IN TERMS OF STUFFING YOUR FACE WITH FOOD COOKED ON THE BARBECUE, EXPENSIVE SEAFOOD IS THE ABSOLUTE PINNACLE OF SOPHISTICATION, REFINEMENT, AND DECADENCE. THESE ARE OBVIOUSLY TERMS THAT DESCRIBE YOU PERFECTLY, SO HERE'S A RECIPE FOR SCALLOPS WITH A LIME AND CHILE MARINADE AND A COCONUT DRESSING. THIS IS JUST A SUGGESTION, BUT THE WHOLE EXPERIENCE WILL BE MUCH ENHANCED IF YOU INVEST IN A WHITE TUXEDO TO WEAR WHILE BARBECUING AND EATING THEM.

24 large scallops, without corals

2 tablespoons peanut oil

grated zest of 2 unwaxed limes

2 fresh red chile peppers, such as serrano, seeded and chopped

2 teaspoons grated fresh ginger

1 garlic clove, crushed

1 tablespoon Thai fish sauce

coconut milk dressing

⅓ cup (125 ml) coconut milk

1 tablespoon Thai fish sauce

2 teaspoons sugar

2 teaspoons coconut or rice wine vinegar

serves 6

★ Trim the tough white muscle from the side of each scallop. Put the scallops into a shallow non-metal dish.

★ Put the peanut oil, lime zest, chiles, ginger, garlic, and fish sauce into a small pitcher (jug) or bowl, mix well, then pour over the scallops. Let marinate in the refrigerator for 1 hour.

★ To make the dressing, put the coconut milk, fish sauce, sugar, and vinegar into a small pan, heat gently to dissolve the sugar, then bring to a gentle simmer until thickened slightly. Remove from the heat and let cool completely.

★ Meanwhile, preheat the grill/barbecue until hot. Thread the scallops onto the prepared skewers and cook for 1 minute on each side. Don't overcook, or the scallops will be tough. Serve with the coconut dressing and wedges of lime.

SOUK KEBABS
with roasted cumin and paprika

IF YOU'VE EVER VISITED MARRAKECH, YOU'LL KNOW THAT THE BEST FOOD TO BE HAD IS FROM THE STREET VENDORS. FORGET THE RESTAURANTS, IT'S ALL ABOUT SIMPLE "HOLE IN THE WALL," ONE-MAN-AND-A-CHARCOAL-GRILL SETUPS. DIRT CHEAP AND ABSOLUTELY DELICIOUS, KEBABS LIKE THESE ARE SOLD EVERYWHERE. FIRE THEM ON THE BARBECUE AND EAT THEM STRAIGHT OFF THE SKEWER, OR, IF YOU'RE FEELING A BIT GREEDY, WRAP THEM IN FLATBREAD WITH TOMATO SALSA OR HARISSA.

★ Put the grated onion in a bowl and sprinkle with the sea salt. Set aside to "weep" for 10 minutes, then force it through a nylon strainer (sieve), or squeeze it with your hand, to extract the juice.

★ Put the lamb in a bowl and pour over the extracted onion juice. Add the lemon juice, roasted cumin, paprika, herbs, and black pepper, to taste. Toss well so that the meat is thoroughly coated in the marinade. Cover and chill in the refrigerator for at least 2 hours, or overnight, to allow the flavors to penetrate the meat.

★ Prepare the grill/barbecue. Thread the marinated meat onto skewers, grill for 3–4 minutes on each side until cooked through, and serve immediately with wedges of lemon to squeeze over them.

1–2 onions, grated

2 teaspoons sea salt

1 lb. (500 g) lean shoulder of lamb, trimmed and cut into bite-size cubes

freshly squeezed juice of 1 lemon

2 teaspoons cumin seeds, roasted and ground

1–2 teaspoons paprika

a small bunch of fresh flat leaf parsley, finely chopped

a small bunch of fresh cilantro (coriander), finely chopped

freshly ground black pepper

1 lemon, cut into wedges, to serve

serves 4

CHICKEN KEBABS MOROCCAN STYLE

YOU CAN'T BEAT THE HEAVILY SPICED FLAVORS OF MOROCCAN STREET FOOD. HERE, CHICKEN IS MARINATED OVERNIGHT IN A CLASSIC MIX OF NORTH AFRICAN SPICES AND COOKED QUICKLY ON THE BARBECUE (NOT TOO QUICKLY, MIND; ALWAYS AVOID PINK CHICKEN!). THE SMELL OF THE SPICED MEAT COOKING IS ABSOLUTELY BANGING. SERVE THESE WITH A SQUEEZE OF LEMON, CHARGRILLED FLATBREAD, AND A BOWL OF YOGURT ON THE SIDE FOR DIPPING.

1 lb. (500 g) skinless, boneless chicken breasts

2 tablespoons extra virgin olive oil

juice of 1 large lemon

1 tablespoon chopped fresh thyme leaves

2 garlic cloves, crushed

1 teaspoon ground turmeric

1 teaspoon ground cinnamon

½ teaspoon ground allspice

½ teaspoon salt

¼ teaspoon ground cayenne pepper

lemon wedges, to serve

plain yogurt, to serve

serves 4

★ Cut the chicken lengthways into ⅛-inch (3-mm) strips and put into a shallow ceramic dish. Put the oil, lemon juice, thyme, garlic, turmeric, cinnamon, allspice, salt, and cayenne into a pitcher (jug), mix well, then pour over the chicken. Cover and marinate overnight in the refrigerator.

★ The next day, return to room temperature for 1 hour. Thread the strips onto skewers, zigzagging back and forth. Cook on a preheated grill/barbecue for 3–4 minutes on each side until charred and cooked through. Serve with lemon wedges and yogurt.

CHICKEN TANDOORI KEBABS

2 lb. (1 kg) skinless, boneless chicken breasts, cut into bite-size pieces

2 tablespoons ghee or butter, melted

marinade

3 fresh red or green chile peppers, seeded and chopped

2–3 garlic cloves, chopped

1-inch (2.5-cm) piece fresh ginger, peeled and chopped

2 tablespoons heavy (double) cream

3 tablespoons vegetable oil

1 tablespoon paprika

2 teaspoons ground cumin

2 teaspoons ground cardamom

1 teaspoon ground cloves

1 teaspoon sea salt

to serve

crispy poppadoms

tomato and cucumber salad

limes wedges (optional)

serves 4

I'M GUESSING THAT, LIKE ME, YOU PROBABLY DON'T HAVE A TRADITIONAL TANDOORI OVEN KNOCKING AROUND IN THE KITCHEN. IF YOU'RE SCRATCHING YOUR HEAD, WONDERING HOW THE HELL YOU CAN GO ABOUT REPRODUCING THIS CLASSIC INDIAN RECIPE WITHOUT THE REQUIRED KIT, STOP WORRYING. BELIEVE IT OR NOT, A REGULAR BARBECUE WORKS JUST FINE AS A SUBSTITUTE. THESE KEBABS TAKE 48 HOURS TO MARINATE PROPERLY, SO PREP THEM WELL IN ADVANCE; BELIEVE ME, THE RESULT IS WORTH IT. SERVE WITH A FRESH TOMATO AND CUCUMBER SALAD.

★ To prepare the marinade, use a mortar and pestle, or a food processor, to mince the chiles, garlic, and ginger to a paste. Beat in the cream and oil with 3–4 tablespoons water to form a smooth mixture. Beat in the dried spices.

★ Place the chicken pieces in a bowl and rub with the marinade until thoroughly coated. Cover and chill in the refrigerator for about 48 hours. Lift the chicken pieces out of the marinade and thread them onto skewers. Prepare the grill/barbecue. Brush the chicken with the melted ghee and grill for 3–4 minutes on each side. Serve with crispy poppadoms, a salad of finely diced tomato, cucumber, and onion with fresh cilantro (coriander), and wedges of lime for squeezing, if liked.

pickled cucumber

1 lb. (500 g) pickling cucumbers

1 tablespoon Kosher (table) salt

2 teaspoons brown sugar

½ teaspoon black peppercorns

½ teaspoon pink peppercorns

1 teaspoon yellow mustard seeds

4 fresh bay leaves

1½ cups (350 ml) apple cider vinegar

1 sterilized quart (liter) glass jar with lid

rub

½ preserved lemon, finely chopped

1 tablespoon dried mint

2 tablespoons fresh lemon juice

fresh thyme leaves

1 tablespoon fresh rosemary leaves

¼ cup (60 ml) extra virgin olive oil

freshly squeezed juice and grated zest of 1 unwaxed lemon

sea salt and coarsely ground black pepper

kebabs

1½ lb. (750 g) lamb shoulder

1 lemon

6 fresh bay leaves

coarsely ground black pepper

serves 6

Mint and lemon thyme

LAMB KEBABS with pickled cucumber

THIS IS A CRACKING RECIPE, USING LAMB SHOULDER (LEG WORKS WELL TOO), SERVED WITH PICKLED CUCUMBER. IF YOU'RE FEELING ORGANIC AND YOU'RE LUCKY ENOUGH TO HAVE A FLOURISHING ROSEMARY BUSH, YOU CAN USE THE BRANCHES FOR SKEWERS.

★ For the pickled cucumber, in a nonreactive pan add the salt, sugar, peppercorns, mustard seeds, bay leaves, cider vinegar, and ¼ cup (60 ml) water. Bring to a boil over a medium–high heat, then reduce the heat to medium and simmer until the salt and sugar have dissolved.

★ Cut the cucumbers into spears and pack them into the glass jar. Pour the hot pickling juice over the cucumbers and fill to the top. Screw the lid on and let cool completely before placing in the refrigerator. They will keep for 2 weeks.

★ For the rub, put all the ingredients in a bowl and mix together. Season to taste with salt and pepper and use immediately.

★ Rinse the lamb under cold running water and pat dry with paper towels (kitchen paper). Cut the lamb into 1¼-inch (3-cm) cubes and put in a mixing bowl. Sprinkle the rub over the lamb and toss to coat evenly. Season with cracked black pepper. (The salt from the preserved lemon should be enough to season.) Cover and refrigerate for 8–24 hours.

★ Slice the lemon in half, then cut each half into half moons. Remove the lamb from the fridge and, while still cold, thread onto pre-soaked wooden skewers or rosemary branches, along with the bay leaves and lemon slices. Cover the skewers and allow to come to room temperature.

★ On a medium–high grill/barbecue, cook the lamb skewers for 5 minutes, then reduce the heat to medium and turn. Cook for a further 6–8 minutes, turning frequently to make sure all the sides are brown and crispy. If you prefer your meat well done, continue to cook the skewers to your preference. Serve with the pickled cucumber.

LAMB AND PORCINI KEBABS
with sage and Parmesan

BEAUTIFUL ITALIAN FLAVORS OF SAGE, PORCINI MUSHROOM, AND PARMESAN ARE USED HERE TO COMPLEMENT CHUNKS OF CHARGRILLED LAMB. THE RECIPE CALLS FOR FRESH PORCINI, WHICH—UNLESS YOU LIVE IN RURAL ITALY—ISN'T THE EASIEST (OR CHEAPEST) THING TO OBTAIN, SO USE THE DRIED VARIETY (RECONSTITUTING IT IN WATER). JUST MAKE SURE YOU GET A PACKAGE WITH LARGE PIECES IN, AND NOT A BAG OF DRIED DUST ... GOOD LUCK WITH THREADING THAT ONTO A SKEWER! OTHERWISE, USE CHESTNUT MUSHROOMS. LOVELY STUFF.

1 lb. (500 g) tender lamb, from the leg or shoulder, cut into bite-size chunks

2 tablespoons olive oil

freshly squeezed juice of 1–2 lemons

leaves from a bunch of fresh sage, finely chopped (reserve a few whole leaves)

2 garlic cloves, crushed

sea salt and freshly ground black pepper

4–8 fresh medium-sized porcini, cut into quarters or thickly sliced

to serve

truffle oil, to drizzle

Parmesan cheese shavings

grilled or toasted sourdough bread

serves 4

★ Put the lamb pieces in a bowl and toss in the oil and lemon juice. Add the sage and garlic and season with salt and pepper. Cover, refrigerate, and leave to marinate for about 2 hours.

★ Thread the lamb onto skewers adding a quarter, or slice, of porcini every so often with a sage leaf. Brush with any of the marinade left in the bowl. Prepare the grill/barbecue. Cook the kebabs for 3–4 minutes on each side.

★ Serve immediately with a drizzle of truffle oil, Parmesan shavings, and toasted sourdough bread, if liked.

SPICY BEEF AND COCONUT KOFTA KEBABS

THIS IS AN INCREDIBLY QUICK, EASY, AND CHEAP RECIPE TO THROW TOGETHER, TAKING NO TIME AT ALL TO PREPARE AND TO COOK ON THE BARBECUE. THIS CLASSIC COMBINATION OF BEEF AND COCONUT IS FOUND THROUGHOUT ASIA IN ONE FORM OR ANOTHER ON STREET STALLS. SERVE WITH FRESH LIME SQUEEZED OVER, AND MAYBE SOME KIND OF CHILE DIPPING SAUCE ON THE SIDE, IF YOU FANCY A BIT OF HEAT.

1 teaspoon coriander seeds

1 teaspoon cumin seeds

1⅓ cups (175 g) dried shredded (desiccated) or freshly grated coconut, plus 2–3 tablespoons, to serve

1 tablespoon coconut oil

4 shallots, peeled and finely chopped

2 garlic cloves, finely chopped

1–2 fresh red chile peppers, seeded and finely chopped

12 oz. (350 g) lean ground (minced) beef

1 beaten egg, to bind

sea salt and freshly ground black pepper

lime wedges, to serve

serves 4

★ In a small heavy-based skillet or frying pan, dry roast the coriander and cumin seeds until they give off a nutty aroma. Using a mortar and pestle, or a spice grinder, grind the roasted seeds to a powder.

★ In the same pan, dry roast the coconut until it begins to color and give off a nutty aroma. Tip it onto a plate to cool, reserving 2–3 tablespoons.

★ Heat the coconut oil in the same pan and stir in the shallots, garlic, and chiles, until fragrant and beginning to color. Tip them onto a plate to cool.

★ Put the ground (minced) beef in a bowl and add the ground spices, toasted coconut, and shallot mixture. Season with salt and pepper and use a fork to mix all the ingredients together, adding a little egg to bind it (you may not need it all). Knead the mixture with your hands and mold it into little balls. Thread the balls onto the prepared skewers.

★ Prepare the grill/barbecue. Cook the kebabs for 3–4 minutes on each side. Sprinkle the cooked kofta with the reserved toasted coconut and serve with the wedges of lime to squeeze over them.

YOU'LL FIND THIS TYPE OF KEBAB THROUGHOUT THE MIDDLE EAST AND NORTH AFRICA. CUMIN-SPICED LAMB, FIRED QUICKLY OVER COALS, SLICED, AND SERVED WITH CREAMY HUMMUS, SALAD, AND FLATBREADS. ABSOLUTELY DELICIOUS. TO MAKE THESE KEBABS SUCCESSFULLY, YOU'LL NEED A COUPLE LARGE METAL SKEWERS WITH WIDE, FLAT BLADES TO HOLD THE MEAT.

LAMB KEBABS

with roasted cumin and hummus

1 lb. (500 g) finely ground (minced) lean lamb

1 onion, grated

2 teaspoons ground cumin

1 teaspoon ground coriander

1 teaspoon paprika

½–1 teaspoon cayenne pepper

1 teaspoon sea salt

a small bunch of fresh flat leaf parsley, finely chopped

a small bunch of fresh cilantro (coriander), finely chopped

leafy herb salad, to serve

flatbreads, to serve

hot hummus

1½ cups (300 g) dried chickpeas, soaked overnight and cooked in plenty of water until tender, or a 14-oz. (400-g) can cooked chickpeas, drained

3 tablespoons olive oil

freshly squeezed juice of 1 lemon

1 teaspoon cumin seeds

2 tablespoons light tahini

4 tablespoons thick, strained plain (Greek) yogurt

sea salt and freshly ground black pepper

2½ tablespoons butter

serves 4–6

★ Mix the ground (minced) lamb with the other ingredients and knead well. Pound the meat to a smooth consistency in a large mortar and pestle, or whizz in a food processor. Leave to sit for 1 hour to let the flavors mingle.

★ Meanwhile, make the hummus. Preheat the oven to 400°F (200°C). In a food processor, whizz the chickpeas with the olive oil, lemon juice, cumin seeds, tahini, and yogurt. Season to taste, tip the mixture into an ovenproof dish, cover with foil, and put in the preheated oven to warm through.

★ Wet your hands to make the meat mixture easier to handle. Mold portions of the mixture around the skewers, squeezing and flattening it, so it looks like the sheath to a sword.

★ Preheat the grill/barbecue. Cook the kebabs for 4–5 minutes on each side. Quickly melt the butter in a pan or in the microwave and pour it over the hummus. When the kebabs are cooked on both sides, slip the meat off the skewers, cut into bite-size pieces, and serve with the hot hummus, a leafy herb salad, and flatbreads on the side.

DUCK YAKITORI

IN JAPAN, YAKITORI (SKEWERED CHICKEN KEBABS) ARE TRADITIONALLY SERVED IN SMALL, INFORMAL RESTAURANTS OR STREET STANDS, GRILLED TO ORDER OVER CHARCOAL AND WASHED DOWN WITH BEER. WHAT AN ABSOLUTELY PERFECT WAY TO SPEND AN EVENING. THIS RECIPE MOVES THINGS UP A NOTCH BY USING DUCK BREAST, MARINATED IN A SWEET SOY AND SAKE SAUCE AND SERVED WITH SOBA NOODLES AND A CUCUMBER CHILE SALAD ON THE SIDE. LOVELY.

6 tablespoons Japanese soy sauce

3 tablespoons sake

2 tablespoons sugar

4 small duck breast fillets, about 5 oz. (150 g) each, skinned

soba noodles, cooked according to the package instructions, then drained and chilled, to serve

cucumber salad

2 tablespoons rice vinegar

2 tablespoons sugar

½ cucumber, about 8 inches (20 cm), finely sliced

1 fresh red chile pepper, seeded and chopped

serves 4

★ Put the soy sauce, sake, and sugar into a small pan and heat gently to dissolve the sugar. Cool completely.

★ Cut the duck lengthwise into ⅛-inch (3-mm) strips and put into a shallow ceramic dish. Pour over the soy sauce mixture and marinate in the refrigerator for 2–4 hours or overnight.

★ Just before cooking the duck, prepare the salad. Put the vinegar, sugar, and 2 tablespoons water into a small pan, heat to dissolve the sugar, then let cool. Stir in the cucumber and chile and set aside.

★ Thread the duck strips onto skewers, zigzagging back and forth. Cook on a preheated grill/barbecue for 2 minutes on each side until cooked through. Serve with chilled soba noodles and the cucumber salad.

CHARGRILLED TAMARIND SHRIMP

AS EVERYONE KNOWS, THE SIZE OF YOUR SHRIMP (PRAWN) IS A GOOD MEASURE OF THE QUALITY OF YOUR LIFE. BEARING THIS IN MIND, I ADVISE YOU TO USE THE BIGGEST, MOST RIDICULOUSLY MASSIVE SHRIMP YOU CAN FIND FOR THIS RECIPE. THESE CHARCOAL-GRILLED TAMARIND SHRIMP ARE AN INCREDIBLY POPULAR STREET FOOD IN BOTH MALAYSIA AND INDONESIA. IT'S NOT SURPRISING—SEAFOOD COOKED SIMPLY ON THE BARBECUE IS PRETTY MUCH UNBEATABLE.

1 lb. (500 g) shrimp (prawns), deveined and trimmed of heads, feelers, and legs

leaves from a small bunch of fresh cilantro (coriander), to serve

2–4 fresh green chile peppers, seeded and sliced, to serve

marinade

3 tablespoons tamarind pulp

2 tablespoons sweet soy sauce

1 tablespoon sugar

freshly ground black pepper

serves 2–4

★ Rinse the prepared shrimp (prawns) well, pat dry, and, using a very sharp knife, make an incision along the curve of the tail. Set aside.

★ Put the tamarind pulp in a bowl and add 1 cup (240 ml) warm water. Soak the pulp until soft, squeezing it with your fingers to help dissolve it. Strain the liquid and discard any fiber or seeds. In a bowl, mix the tamarind juice, soy sauce, sugar, and black pepper. Pour it over the shrimp, rubbing it over the shells and into the incision in the tails. Cover, refrigerate, and leave to marinate for about 1 hour.

★ Preheat the grill/barbecue. Insert a skewer into each marinated shrimp. Cook the shrimp for about 3 minutes on each side, until the shells have turned orange, brushing them with extra marinade as they cook. Serve immediately, garnished with the cilantro (coriander) and chiles.

NOTE Tamarind lends a rich, sweet-sour flavor to dishes. The tropical trees produce fresh pods that are either sold fresh or processed into pulp or paste for convenience and long shelf life. Look out for it in Asian or Caribbean stores— semi-dried tamarind pulp comes in soft rectangular blocks sealed in plastic wrap (clingfilm). The darker concentrated paste is sold in tubs and is a more processed product.

CHERRY POMEGRANATE GRILLED DUCK SKEWERS

DUCK AND CHERRIES IS AN ABSOLUTE CLASSIC COMBINATION. THE SWEET, SLIGHTLY TART FRUIT COMPLEMENTS THE RICHNESS OF THE MEAT PERFECTLY. THE ADDITION OF POMEGRANATE ADDS A SWEET MIDDLE EASTERN VIBE TO THE PROCEEDINGS. DUCK ISN'T THE CHEAPEST FORM OF PROTEIN, SO I'D CONSIDER THESE SKEWERS LESS WEEK-NIGHT DINNER AND MORE IMPRESS-THE-GUESTS, DRINKS-PARTY-TYPE GRUB. THESE WOULD BE GREAT SERVED WITH CHARGRILLED PITA AND A HERBY SALAD, SUCH AS TABBOULEH.

glaze

2 cups (450 g) dark cherries (such as Bing cherries), pitted

2 tablespoons pomegranate molasses

2 teaspoons dried thyme

2 teaspoons dried rosemary

sea salt and freshly ground black pepper

2 duck breasts (about 1 lb./500 g)

makes 16 skewers

★ For the glaze, put the cherries and pomegranate molasses in a food processor and pulse until you have a chunky sauce. Pour the sauce into a ceramic bowl and stir in the thyme and rosemary. Season with salt and pepper. Store in an airtight container and keep in the fridge for up to 2 weeks.

★ Wash the duck breasts in cold water and pat dry with paper towels (kitchen paper). Put the duck on a board and slice crosswise into 1½-inch (4-cm) strips.

★ Pour the glaze into a large glass bowl and add the duck strips. Stir well to make sure the duck is completely covered in the marinade, then cover and refrigerate overnight.

★ Remove the duck from the fridge. While the strips are still cold, thread them onto 16 pre-soaked wooden skewers, cover, and set aside until they come up to room temperature.

★ Pour the remaining marinade into a small pan and bring to a boil. Reduce the heat and simmer the sauce for 10 minutes.

★ Lay the duck skewers, fat side down, on a medium–high grill/barbecue. Cook for 5 minutes, then turn over. Reduce the heat to medium and cook for a further 5 minutes, until crispy on the outside and cooked through. Pour the warm marinade into a small bowl and serve with the skewers.

PORTERHOUSE STEAK
with chimichurri

IF YOU WANT TO FEEL LIKE YOU'VE REALLY MASTERED THE BARBECUE THING, YOU NEED TO COOK A WHOPPING PIECE OF STEAK ON THE GRILL, A PIECE OF MEAT SO BIG THAT IT'LL COMFORTABLY FEED FOUR PEOPLE. THIS RECIPE CALLS FOR A 2-INCH-THICK PORTERHOUSE STEAK. YEAH, IT'S PRACTICALLY HALF A COW, BUT DON'T LET THAT PUT YOU OFF. WE'RE GOING TO SERVE IT WITH CHIMICHURRI SAUCE, A HERBY GREEN SAUCE FROM ARGENTINA THAT IS GORGEOUS WITH STEAK. AIM FOR RARE OR MEDIUM RARE. WELL DONE IS FOR LOSERS.

* Remove the steak from the fridge and let it come to room temperature.

* Drizzle the meat with olive oil and sprinkle generously on both sides with the salt and pepper.

* Prepare a medium–high grill/barbecue. Place the steak on the grill and cook for 8–10 minutes on each side for rare; continue to cook if you prefer medium to well done.

* Remove the steak from the grill, cover, and let it rest for 10 minutes. Carve and serve with the Chimichurri sauce.

1 large Porterhouse steak, 2 inches (5 cm) thick

2 tablespoons olive oil

sea salt and coarsely ground black pepper

1 recipe of Chimichurri (see opposite), to serve

serves 4

CHIMICHURRI

a small bunch of fresh oregano leaves

a small bunch of fresh marjoram leaves

a bunch of fresh flat leaf parsley leaves

1 small red jalapeño pepper, finely chopped

2 garlic cloves, finely chopped

½ cup (120 ml) red wine vinegar

1 cup (240 ml) extra virgin olive oil

coarsely ground black pepper

makes about 2 cups (450 ml)

★ Put the oregano, marjoram, and parsley on a wooden board and finely chop. Put the jalapeño and garlic in a ceramic bowl along with the chopped herbs. Pour in the red wine vinegar and olive oil, stir well, and season to taste with salt and pepper.

★ Cover and leave in the fridge until ready to use, so the flavors can mingle, then bring to room temperature when ready to serve.

GRILLED SKIRT STEAK
with smoked butter

- -

SKIRT STEAK IS A SUPERB CUT OF MEAT, FULL OF FLAVOR BUT TOUGH AS OLD BOOTS UNLESS IT'S MARINATED FIRST. HERE IT'S RUBBED WITH AN AFRICAN SPICE MIX AND LEFT OVERNIGHT TO TENDERIZE, THEN FIRED QUICKLY ON THE GRILL. PLUCK IT STRAIGHT OFF THE BARBECUE, SQUASH IT INTO A BAGUETTE WITH SMOKED BUTTER AND WATERCRESS, AND STUFF IT INTO YOUR FACE. HOW GOOD DOES THAT SOUND?

rub

1 teaspoon smoked sea salt

1 teaspoon ground garlic powder

1 teaspoon ground black pepper

1 tablespoon dried chili flakes

1 teaspoon fenugreek seeds

2 dried bay leaves

smoked butter

2½ teaspoons smoked sea salt

2 sticks (225 g) unsalted butter, at room temperature

cracked black pepper

steak

1 lb. (500 g) skirt steak

olive oil, to drizzle

to serve

a rustic baguette

smoked butter

2 cups (100 g) watercress sprigs

serves 4–6

★ For the rub, put all the ingredients into an electric spice grinder and process to a coarse powder. You can store the rub in a glass jar with a tight-fitting lid for up to 6 months.

★ For the smoked butter, put the salt and butter in a food processor and process until smooth. Season with pepper and refrigerate until ready to use.

★ Rinse the skirt steak under cold water and pat dry with paper towels (kitchen paper). Put in a ceramic dish and drizzle with a little olive oil. Sprinkle the rub over both sides of the steak. Season with cracked black pepper, then cover and refrigerate overnight.

★ Remove the steak from the fridge and let it come to room temperature.

★ Prepare a hot grill/barbecue. Put the steak on the grill and cook for 4–5 minutes on each side. If you prefer your steak well done, continue to cook it for a few more minutes.

★ Cut the baguette in half and toast on the grill, then spread with some smoked butter. Lay the steak on the bottom half of the baguette, sprinkle over the watercress sprigs, and top with the lid. Cut into thick slices and serve.

SIMPLE PSYCHO RIBS

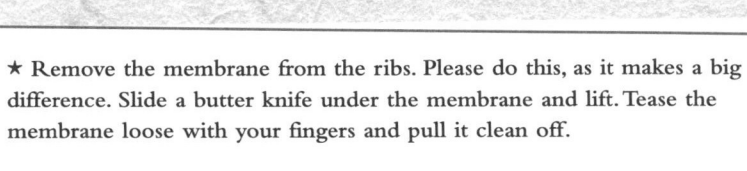

FIRST OF ALL, DON'T BE PUT OFF BY THE OMINOUS "PSYCHO" IN THE TITLE OF THIS RECIPE; IT REFERS TO A PARTICULAR BRAND OF HOT SAUCE. BARBECUED BABY BACK RIBS CAN BE ABSOLUTELY INCREDIBLE. THEY ARE OFTEN COOKED IN A SMOKER, BUT HERE THEY ARE COATED IN A DRY RUB, THEN FOILED AND COOKED IN A LOW OVEN FOR 4 HOURS BEFORE BEING FINISHED OFF QUICKLY ON A GRILL OR BARBECUE. THEY'RE FANTASTIC SERVED WITH A HEAP OF HOMEMADE 'SLAW. FEEL FREE TO CUT DOWN ON THE CHILI INGREDIENTS IN THE RUB, IF YOU THINK IT'S A BIT TOO HOT.

3 lb. (1.5 kg) pork baby back ribs

2 tablespoons vegetable oil

rub

2 tablespoons cayenne pepper

1 tablespoon chipotle chili powder

2 tablespoons brown sugar

2 tablespoons superfine (caster) sugar

2 tablespoons paprika

1 tablespoon garlic powder

1 tablespoon salt

½ tablespoon ground black pepper

½ tablespoon ground ginger

½ tablespoon dried onion powder

½ tablespoon rosemary powder

baste

1 tablespoon smoked hot sauce (ideally Psycho Juice Smoked Ghost Pepper)

2 cups (450 ml) barbecue sauce

serves 4

★ Remove the membrane from the ribs. Please do this, as it makes a big difference. Slide a butter knife under the membrane and lift. Tease the membrane loose with your fingers and pull it clean off.

★ Combine all the ingredients for the rub in a bowl.

★ Rub the ribs with vegetable oil. Sprinkle both sides of the ribs with the rub. Wrap the ribs in foil and put in the fridge for at least an hour or two, overnight if possible.

★ Preheat the oven to 275°F (135°C) and cook the ribs low and slow in their foil for about 4 hours.

★ Mix the hot sauce with the barbecue sauce.

★ Prepare a hot grill/barbecue. Remove the ribs from the foil and grill them for 5–10 minutes while brushing with the barbecue sauce until well colored and caramelized.

BARBECUE SPARERIBS
with Mexican salsa

2 garlic cloves, crushed

2 tablespoons sea salt

2 tablespoons ground cumin

1 teaspoon Tabasco sauce

1 teaspoon dried oregano

½ cup (125 ml) honey

4 tablespoons sherry vinegar

6 tablespoons olive oil

2 lb. (1 kg) barbecue pork spareribs

salsa

2 corn cobs, husks removed, brushed with corn oil

2 red bell peppers, quartered and seeded

2 long fresh red chiles, such as New Mexico, halved and seeded

4 ripe red tomatoes, halved, seeded, and finely diced

1 red onion, chopped

2 garlic cloves, crushed

2 tablespoons chopped or torn fresh cilantro (coriander)

dressing

½ teaspoon sugar

1 tablespoon corn oil

freshly squeezed juice of 1 lime

1 teaspoon sea salt, or to taste

freshly ground black pepper

serves 4

WHEN KNOCKING UP A SALSA IN MEXICO, COOKS OFTEN GRILL THE INGREDIENTS FIRST. CORN, CHILES, BELL PEPPERS, AND EVEN TOMATOES ARE ALL GIVEN A QUICK TURN OVER THE FLAMES, TO GET THAT SMOKY BARBECUE FLAVOR RUNNING THROUGH EVERYTHING. LOVELY. SERVE THIS CRACKING SALSA WITH THE SWEET PORK SPARERIBS, COOKED SLOWLY OVER A MEDIUM BARBECUE.

★ To make a marinade for the spareribs, put the garlic, salt, cumin, Tabasco, oregano, honey, vinegar, and olive oil into a shallow dish and mix. Pat the ribs dry with paper towels (kitchen paper), add them to the dish, then rub in the marinade. Cover and chill overnight.

★ Put the corn, pepper quarters, and chile halves onto a preheated grill/barbecue or under the broiler (grill). Toast until the pepper and chile skins and the corn are all lightly charred. Cool, then pull off the pepper and chile skins (leaving a few charred bits behind) and slice the kernels off the corn cobs. Put into a bowl, add the tomatoes, onion, and garlic, then toss well.

★ To make the dressing for the salsa, put the sugar, corn oil, lime juice, salt, and pepper into a bowl or pitcher, mix well, then pour over the vegetables and toss again. Cover and chill for at least 30 minutes. Before serving, stir through the chopped or torn cilantro (coriander). Taste and add extra salt and freshly cracked black pepper if necessary.

★ When ready to cook, prepare a medium–high grill/barbecue, then add the ribs and cook on both sides for about 30 minutes until done. Baste from time to time with the marinade.

★ Cut the ribs into slices, each side of the bones, and arrange on 4 serving plates. Serve with the salsa beside or in a separate bowl. Have lots of napkins for mopping up, plus lots of cold beer.

RIB EYE STEAK
with anchovy butter

IF YOU ASKED ME WHAT MY FAVORITE CUT OF STEAK WAS, I'D HAVE TO SAY RIB EYE. IT JUST TASTES SO GOOD, THANKS TO THE MARBLING OF FAT THROUGHOUT THE CUT. COOKED OVER COALS ON THE BARBECUE, IT'S GOT TO BE ONE OF THE BEST THINGS YOU'LL EVER STICK IN YOUR MOUTH, PERIOD. HERE IT'S FIRED ON THE GRILL AND LEFT TO REST BEFORE SERVING, WITH ANCHOVY BUTTER MELTING AND DRIBBLING ALL OVER THE MEAT. SEXUAL. COOK RARE OR MEDIUM. IF YOU COOK IT WELL DONE, YOU'LL GO TO CULINARY HELL.

1¼ sticks (150 g) butter, softened

8 anchovy fillets in oil, drained and coarsely chopped

2 tablespoons chopped fresh flat leaf parsley

4 Delmonico (rib eye) steaks, about 8 oz. (225 g) each

oil, for brushing

sea salt and freshly ground black pepper

serves 4

★ Put the butter, anchovies, parsley, and a little pepper in a bowl and beat well. Transfer to a sheet of foil and roll up into a log. Chill until needed.

★ Prepare a hot grill/barbecue and brush the rack with oil. Season the steaks with salt and pepper and cook for 3 minutes on each side for rare, 4–5 minutes for medium, and 5–6 minutes for well done.

★ Transfer the steaks to a warmed serving plate and top each one with 2 slices of the anchovy butter. Let rest for about 5 minutes before serving in order to set the juices.

VIETNAMESE PORK BALLS

VIETNAMESE STREET FOOD IS RENOWNED FOR BEING AMONG THE BEST IN THE WORLD. HERE, PORK IS FLAVORED WITH KAFFIR LIME LEAVES, GARLIC, GINGER, CHILE, AND FISH SAUCE, THEN SHAPED INTO BALLS BEFORE BEING QUICKLY COOKED OVER THE BARBECUE ON SKEWERS. SERVE THEM WRAPPED UP IN A LETTUCE LEAF WITH HERBS AND SOME SWEET CHILE SAUCE.

1 lemongrass stalk

1 lb. (500 g) ground (minced) pork

⅓ cup (20 g) bread crumbs

6 kaffir lime leaves, very finely sliced

2 garlic cloves, crushed

1-inch (2.5-cm) piece fresh ginger, peeled and grated

1 fresh red hot chile pepper, seeded and chopped

2 tablespoons Thai fish sauce

to serve

lettuce leaves

a handful of fresh herb leaves, such as mint, cilantro (coriander), and Thai basil

Sweet Chile Sauce (page 21)

serves 4

★ Using a sharp knife, trim the lemongrass stalk to about 6 inches (15 cm), then remove and discard the tough outer leaves. Chop the inner stalk very finely.

★ Put the pork and bread crumbs into a bowl, then add the lemongrass, lime leaves, garlic, ginger, chile, and fish sauce and mix well. Let marinate in the refrigerator for at least 1 hour.

★ Using your hands, shape the mixture into 20 small balls and carefully thread 5 each onto 4 pre-soaked wooden skewers. Preheat the grill/barbecue, then brush the grill rack with oil. Cook the skewers over hot coals for 5–6 minutes, turning halfway through, until cooked.

★ Serve the pork balls wrapped in the lettuce leaves with the herbs and Sweet Chile Sauce.

DUCK SATAY
with grilled pineapple and plum sauce

ALONGSIDE THE MORE COMMON CHICKEN, DUCK SATAY IS OFTEN SERVED IN VIETNAM, CAMBODIA, AND CHINA. HERE, THE DUCK IS GRILLED ON THE BARBECUE ALONG WITH SLICES OF PINEAPPLE. YOU MAY BE THINKING THE INCLUSION OF PINEAPPLE IS SOMEHOW A BIT NAFF, LIKE CHEESE AND PINEAPPLE ON STICKS, BUT DON'T WORRY, HERE IT'S USED IN THE CHINESE TRADITION OF SWEET AND SOUR WITH A FRUITY PLUM SAUCE, SO IT'S DEFINITELY OK.

★ To make the marinade, put the soy sauce and lime juice in a bowl with the sugar and mix until it dissolves. Add the garlic, ginger, and grated onion and stir in the ground coriander and salt.

★ Place the strips of duck in a bowl and pour over the marinade. Toss well, cover, and chill in the refrigerator for at least 4 hours. Thread the duck strips onto pre-soaked wooden skewers and brush them with oil.

★ Prepare the grill/barbecue. Cook the satays for 3–4 minutes on each side, until the duck is nicely browned. Grill the slices of pineapple at the same time. When browned, cut them into bite-size pieces and serve with the duck. Serve drizzled with the plum sauce.

1 lb. 9 oz. (725 g) duck breasts or boned thighs, sliced into thin, bite-size strips

1–2 tablespoons groundnut (peanut) or coconut oil, for brushing

1 small pineapple, peeled, cored, and sliced

Chinese plum sauce, to serve

marinade

2–3 tablespoons light soy sauce

freshly squeezed juice of 1 lime

1–2 teaspoons sugar

1–2 garlic cloves, crushed

1-inch (2.5-cm) piece fresh ginger, peeled and grated

1 small onion, grated

1–2 teaspoons ground coriander

1 teaspoon sea salt

serves 4

SAGE-RUBBED PORK CHOPS

PORK AND SAGE IS AN ABSOLUTE CLASSIC FLAVOR COMBINATION. CHOPS ARE A RELATIVELY INEXPENSIVE CUT, AND PERFECT FOR THROWING ON THE BARBECUE. ALTHOUGH NOWADAYS IT'S OK TO SERVE PORK RARE (TRICHINOSIS, THE PARASITIC DISEASE CAUSED BY UNDERCOOKED PORK, ISN'T REALLY A PROBLEM ANYMORE, THANKS TO MODERN FARMING STANDARDS), YOU PROBABLY WANT YOUR PORK COOKED JUST RIGHT, NOT UNDERDONE BUT NOT DRY AND OVERCOOKED EITHER. ONE OF THE BEST CHEFFY WAYS TO TELL IF IT'S PERFECT IS TO PIERCE THE MEAT WITH A METAL SKEWER, LEAVE IT FOR A SECOND, THEN TOUCH IT TO THE SKIN BELOW YOUR BOTTOM LIP. IF IT'S WARM (NOT COLD OR SCORCHING HOT), THEN THE MEAT IS JUST RIGHT. INCIDENTALLY, THIS TEST WORKS WELL FOR COOKING FISH, TOO.

2 tablespoons chopped fresh sage

2 tablespoons whole-grain mustard

2 tablespoons extra virgin olive oil

4 large pork chops

sea salt and freshly ground black pepper

1 recipe Tomato Salsa (page 15), to serve

serves 4

★ Put the sage, mustard, and olive oil into a bowl and mix well. Season with a little salt and pepper, then spread the mixture all over the chops. Let marinate in the refrigerator for 1 hour.

★ Preheat the grill/barbecue, then cook the chops over hot coals for 2½–3 minutes on each side until browned and cooked through. Serve hot, with the fresh tomato salsa.

SPICED PORK BURGER

with satay sauce

1½ lb. (750 g) ground (minced) pork

2 garlic cloves, crushed

1 teaspoon grated fresh ginger

2 tablespoons chopped fresh cilantro (coriander)

2 tablespoons cornstarch (cornflour)

1 egg, lightly beaten

4 hero (oval) rolls

a handful of fresh herbs, such as Thai or plain basil, cilantro (coriander), and mint leaves

sea salt and freshly ground black pepper

peanut (groundnut), safflower, or sunflower oil, for brushing

satay sauce

4 tablespoons chunky (crunchy) peanut butter

2 tablespoons coconut cream

2 tablespoons freshly squeezed lime juice

1 tablespoon sweet chile sauce, plus extra to serve

2 teaspoons light soy sauce

1 teaspoon soft brown sugar

serves 4

I LOVE SATAY SAUCE. I COULD DIP THINGS IN ITS PEANUTTY GOODNESS ALL DAY LONG (OO-ER). HERE IT'S DOLLOPED ON A THAI-SPICED PORK PATTY, GRILLED ON A SKEWER, AND THEN SLID OFF INTO A ROLL (DON'T EAT THE SKEWER, THAT WOULD BE BAD). STUFFED INTO A BUN LIKE THIS, IT'S CERTAINLY NOT AN AUTHENTIC THAI DISH, BUT DON'T WORRY ABOUT THAT. IT TASTES GOOD, AND THAT'S ALL THAT MATTERS.

★ Put the pork, garlic, ginger, cilantro (coriander), cornstarch (cornflour), egg, salt, and pepper to taste in a bowl and work together with your hands until evenly mixed. Divide into 12 portions and shape into small logs. Cover and chill for 30 minutes.

★ Meanwhile, to make the satay sauce, put the peanut butter, coconut cream, lime juice, chile sauce, soy sauce, and brown sugar in a small pan and heat gently, stirring until mixed. Simmer gently for 1–2 minutes until thickened. Set aside to cool.

★ Prepare the grill/barbecue. Thread the patties onto pre-soaked wooden skewers and brush with oil. Grill for 6–8 minutes, turning frequently, until charred on the outside and cooked through. Keep them warm.

★ To serve, split the rolls down the middle, open out, and fill with herbs. Remove the skewers from the pork patties and add the patties to the rolls along with some satay sauce and sweet chile sauce. Serve hot.

CHEESEBURGER

IT'S THE HEIGHT OF SUMMER, AND YOU'RE OUT IN THE GARDEN OVERSEEING A FRANKLY KICK-ASS BARBECUE SESSION. THE BEER IS FLOWING, THERE'S SOPHISTICATED DISCUSSION GOING ON, EVERYONE'S LOOKING SUPER-FINE IN THEIR FLOWING SUMMER DRESSES AND LIGHTWEIGHT LINEN SHIRTS. THIS IS HAPPENING! UNTIL YOU REACH DOWN AND START LOBBING YOUR SUPERMARKET FROZEN BURGER PATTIES ON THE GRILL *NEEDLE SCRATCHING ACROSS IBIZA CHILL SESSION 25* WITH YOUR CHOICE OF NASTY, INFERIOR-QUALITY BURGERS YOU'VE RUINED EVERYTHING, FOOL. DON'T LET THIS HAPPEN TO YOU—USE THIS BANGING CHEESEBURGER RECIPE INSTEAD. HELL YEAH!

1½ lb. (750 g) ground (minced) chuck steak

1 onion, finely chopped

1 garlic clove, crushed

2 teaspoons chopped fresh thyme

4 oz. (125 g) Cheddar cheese, sliced

4 burger buns, halved

4 tablespoons mayonnaise

4 leaves of butterhead lettuce

2 tomatoes, sliced

½ red onion, thinly sliced

sea salt and freshly ground black pepper

olive oil, for brushing

serves 4

★ Put the beef, onion, garlic, thyme, and some salt and pepper in a bowl and work together with your hands until evenly mixed and slightly sticky. Divide into 4 portions and shape into patties. Cover and chill for 30 minutes.

★ Preheat the grill/barbecue. Brush the patties lightly with olive oil and grill for 5 minutes on each side until lightly charred and cooked through. Top the patties with the cheese slices and set under a hot broiler (grill) for 30 seconds until the cheese has melted. Keep them warm.

★ Toast the buns, then spread each base and top with mayonnaise. Add the lettuce leaves, cheese-topped patties, and tomato and onion slices. Add the bun tops and serve hot.

1½ lb. (750 g) ground (minced) chuck steak

1 small red onion, finely chopped

1 garlic clove, crushed

2 teaspoons dried oregano

1½ teaspoons ground cumin

2 burger buns, halved

1 cup (100 g) shredded iceberg lettuce

¼ cup (100 g) grated Cheddar cheese

sea salt and freshly ground black pepper

olive oil, for brushing

chile relish

1 lb. (500 g) tomatoes, coarsely chopped

1 red onion, coarsely chopped

2 garlic cloves, crushed

2–4 jalapeño chile peppers, coarsely chopped

2 tablespoons Worcestershire sauce

1 cup (200 g) soft brown sugar

⅔ cup (150 ml) red wine vinegar

2 teaspoons sea salt

serves 4

OPEN TEX-MEX BURGER
with chile relish

IS THE REGULAR BURGER A BIT TOO PEDESTRIAN FOR YOUR TASTE? FANCY SOMETHING A BIT MORE EXOTIC? WELL, HOW ABOUT NOT ONE, BUT TWO PLACES COMING TOGETHER IN ONE BURGERTASTIC OFFERING. THAT'S RIGHT! THE STATE OF TEXAS AND ITS NEIGHBORING COUNTRY, MEXICO, HAVE COMBINED THEIR CULINARY KNOW-HOW TO PROVIDE YOU WITH THIS TASTY BURGER. WHADDYA MEAN IT'S NOT ENOUGH? WELL, IN THAT CASE, FRIEND, WE'LL THROW IN THIS CARIBBEAN CHILE BURGER VARIATION FOR FREE!

★ To make the chile relish, put the tomatoes, onion, garlic, and chiles in a food processor and blend until smooth. Transfer the mixture to a pan, add the Worcestershire sauce, sugar, vinegar, and the 2 teaspoons of salt. Bring to a boil and simmer gently for 30–40 minutes until the sauce has thickened. Let cool completely and refrigerate until required.

★ Put the beef, onion, garlic, oregano, cumin, and some salt and pepper in a bowl and work together with your hands until slightly sticky and evenly mixed. Divide into 4 portions and shape into patties. Cover and chill for 30 minutes.

★ Preheat the grill/barbecue. Brush the patties lightly with olive oil and cook for 4–5 minutes on each side until lightly charred and cooked through. Keep them warm.

★ Lightly toast the buns. Top each half with shredded lettuce, a patty, grated cheese, and relish. Serve hot.

★ For a Caribbean twist, replace the jalapeños in the relish with 1 Scotch Bonnet chile, seeded and chopped. If you're a wuss, add a layer of avocado to temper the heat. Pussy.

sea salt and freshly ground black pepper

toasted pita bread, to serve

simple salad, to serve

burgers

1 lb. (500 g) ground (minced) lamb (lean is good, but a little fat is better as this helps to create a juicy burger)

1 small onion, finely chopped

½ small eating apple, peeled, cored, and grated

5 sun-dried apricots, finely chopped

1 garlic clove, crushed

1 small fresh red chile pepper, seeded and finely chopped

1½ teaspoons Ras-el-Hanout (Moroccan spice blend)

1 tablespoon pepper jelly (chili jam)

1 tablespoon all-purpose (plain) flour

1 tablespoon sunflower oil

pickled cucumber and yogurt dressing

½ small red onion, thinly sliced

4 tablespoons plain yogurt

a small handful of fresh mint, finely chopped

½ cup (100 g) finely chopped pickled cucumber

a good squeeze of lemon juice

serves 6

MOROCCAN LAMB BURGERS
with pickled cucumber and yogurt dressing

APPARENTLY THE AUTHOR OF THIS RECIPE WAS TOLD BY A FRIEND THAT A LAMB BURGER CAN ALWAYS BE IMPROVED BY ADDING GRATED APPLE. IT SEEMS RANDOM, BUT LET'S GO WITH IT, BECAUSE THIS RECIPE DEFINITELY USES APPLE, SO IT SHOULD BE AMAZING. THERE ARE APRICOTS ADDED TOO, PERHAPS ON A WHIM—WHATEVER. BUT WHAT HAVE YOU GOT TO LOSE BY EATING THIS WEIRD FRUITY MEAT BURGER, EXCEPT THE COST OF THE INGREDIENTS AND PERHAPS THE RESPECT OF YOUR FRIENDS? I'M KIDDING! IT'S NICE! PROBABLY.

★ To make the burgers, put the lamb, onion, apple, apricots, garlic, chile, Ras-el-Hanout, pepper jelly (chili jam), 1 teaspoon salt, and 1 teaspoon pepper in a large bowl. Mix everything together well by mashing it with your hands. Try to mix it evenly and thoroughly without overworking the mixture. It should just hold together.

★ Divide the mixture into 6 pieces and gently press to flatten and form generous burgers. Place the burgers on a lightly floured tray, cover with plastic wrap (clingfilm) and refrigerate for at least 1 hour. The flavors will benefit from being left to meld for longer.

★ Meanwhile, to make the dressing, place the sliced onion in a medium bowl, then pour over enough just-boiled water to cover. Leave for about 30 seconds. Drain and rinse the onion under cold water to refresh. Pat dry on paper towels and season lightly with a little salt. Put the yogurt and mint in a small bowl and mix together well. Add the pickled cucumber, blanched onions, and lemon juice and mix. Cover and refrigerate until you are ready to serve.

★ Prepare a medium–high grill/barbecue. Brush the sunflower oil over the burgers and cook for 6–8 minutes each side, or until they are cooked through. Serve the burgers with toasted pita bread, a simple salad, and the dressing.

1½ lb. (750 g) skinless, boneless chicken breasts, ground (minced)

2 garlic cloves, crushed

1 tablespoon chopped fresh rosemary

freshly grated zest and juice of 1 unwaxed lemon

1 egg yolk

⅓ cup (50 g) dried bread crumbs or matzo meal

1 medium eggplant (aubergine)

2 zucchini (courgettes)

4 slices focaccia

radicchio or arugula (rocket) leaves

sea salt and freshly ground black pepper

olive oil, for brushing

tapenade

⅔ cup (125 g) black olives, pitted

2 anchovies in oil, drained

1 garlic clove, crushed

2 tablespoons capers, rinsed

1 teaspoon Dijon mustard

¼ cup (50 ml) extra virgin olive oil

freshly ground black pepper

serves 4

OPEN CHICKEN BURGER
with grilled vegetables

SO MAYBE IT'S THE HEIGHT OF SUMMER WHEN YOU'RE READING THIS AND YOU'RE THINKING THE EVOCATIVE FLAVORS OF THE MEDITERRANEAN WOULD GO WELL ON THE BARBECUE. WELL, YOU'D DEFINITELY BE RIGHT. THE SUBTLE SMOKINESS OF CHARGRILLED VEGETABLES, THE TEXTURE OF FOCACCIA BREAD, AND THE SALTINESS OF OLIVE TAPENADE COMBINED, OH YEAH! SO WHAT IF YOU'RE BURNT RED RAW AND SPRAWLED IN A DECKCHAIR ON A YELLOWING, THREADBARE LAWN IN SCRANTON. JUST CLOSE YOUR EYES AND IMAGINE. BUT DEFINITELY OPEN THEM AGAIN WHEN IT COMES TO COOKING IT.

★ To make the tapenade, put the olives, anchovies, garlic, capers, mustard, and oil in a food processor and blend to form a fairly smooth paste. Season to taste with pepper. Transfer to a dish, cover, and store in the refrigerator for up to 5 days.

★ Put the chicken, garlic, rosemary, lemon zest and juice, egg yolk, bread crumbs, and some salt and pepper in a food processor and pulse until a smooth consistency. Transfer the mixture to a bowl, cover, and chill for 30 minutes. Divide the mixture into 4 portions and shape into patties.

★ Cut the eggplant (aubergine) into 12 slices and the zucchini (courgettes) into 12 thin strips. Brush with olive oil and season with salt and pepper. Grill/barbecue the vegetables for 2–3 minutes on each side until charred and softened. Keep them warm.

★ Meanwhile, brush the chicken patties lightly with olive oil and grill/barbecue for 5 minutes on each side until lightly charred and cooked through. Keep them warm.

★ Toast the focaccia and top each slice with radicchio or arugula (rocket) leaves, patties, grilled vegetables, and some tapenade. Serve hot.

GRILLED HARISSA CHICKEN

YES, A CHICKEN DRUMSTICK ON THE BARBECUE HAS ITS PLACE, BUT IT'S JUST SO BORING. NO ONE, AND I MEAN NO ONE, WILL RESPECT YOU FOR SERVING THAT UP. BUT HEY, THERE'S A SIMPLE FIX: FIRST TOSS YOUR CHICKEN IN HARISSA, THAT READILY AVAILABLE FIERY NORTH AFRICAN CHILI PASTE, A COUPLE HOURS BEFORE GETTING YOUR BARBECUE GROOVE ON, WRAP 'EM IN SOME CILANTRO (CORIANDER) AND BOB'S YOUR UNCLE. YOU HAVE AN AUTHENTIC MOROCCAN RECIPE, AS SERVED IN RURAL VILLAGES. HELL YEAH, RESPECT RESTORED!

1–2 tablespoons Harissa (see below)

4 tablespoons olive oil

8–12 chicken drumsticks

a large bunch of fresh cilantro (coriander), to serve (optional)

sea salt

serves 4

★ Put the harissa in a bowl and stir in the olive oil until blended. Season with salt, if necessary, and smear the mixture over the chicken. Cover and chill in the refrigerator for about 2 hours.

★ Prepare the grill/barbecue. Place the marinated drumsticks on the grill/barbecue and cook for about 4–5 minutes on each side. Wrap them in cilantro (coriander) to serve, if using, and eat immediately.

8 dried red chilis, seeded

2–3 garlic cloves, finely chopped

½ teaspoon sea salt

1 teaspoon ground cumin

1 teaspoon ground coriander

¼ cup (50 ml) olive oil

makes roughly 4 tablespoons (a little goes a long way)

HARISSA

★ Put the chilis in a bowl and pour over enough warm water to cover them. Let them soak for 1 hour. Drain and squeeze out any excess water. Using a mortar and pestle, pound them to a paste with the garlic and salt (or whizz them in an electric mixer). Beat in the cumin and ground coriander and bind with the olive oil.

★ Store the harissa paste in a sealed jar in the refrigerator with a thin layer of olive oil poured on top. It will keep well for about 1 month.

marinade

2 teaspoons ground allspice

1 tablespoon black peppercorns

1 teaspoon grated nutmeg

1 teaspoon ground cinnamon

1 teaspoon sea salt

3 Scotch Bonnet chile peppers, chopped

10 scallions (spring onions), chopped

½ onion, roughly chopped

4 garlic cloves, sliced

2-inch (5-cm) piece fresh ginger, peeled and chopped

a small bunch of fresh thyme, chopped

4 fresh bay leaves, torn

2 tablespoons molasses (maple syrup or treacle can also work)

⅓ cup (80 ml) freshly squeezed lime juice

⅓ cup (80 ml) sunflower oil

1 tablespoon dark rum

chicken

4 chicken breasts, skin on

⅔ cup (150 ml) marinade

1 lime, ½ thinly sliced and ½ freshly squeezed

1 tablespoon dark rum

1 teaspoon dark soy sauce

1 teaspoon dark brown sugar

½ pineapple, peeled, cored and cut into wedges

groundnut (peanut) oil, for greasing (optional)

a salsa of your choice (page 15), to serve

rice salad, to serve

serves 4

JERK CHICKEN
with lime and caramelized pineapple

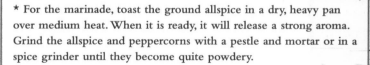

★ For the marinade, toast the ground allspice in a dry, heavy pan over medium heat. When it is ready, it will release a strong aroma. Grind the allspice and peppercorns with a pestle and mortar or in a spice grinder until they become quite powdery.

★ Blend all the ingredients in a food processor to form a smooth, thick paste. Place in a clean, airtight container and refrigerate. The flavor of the marinade will improve over time.

★ Put the chicken in a bowl and cover with the Jamaican jerk marinade. Make sure the chicken is thoroughly coated, then cover and marinate in the refrigerator for at least 2 hours; overnight is ideal.

★ Remove the chicken from the marinade (reserve the marinade). Gently lift the edge of the skin on each chicken breast, creating a small pocket against the flesh. Take 1–2 thin slices of lime (1 for a small piece of chicken, and 2 for a large) and slide these under the skin. They will caramelize during cooking.

★ Prepare a medium grill/barbecue and cook the chicken, basting regularly, for about 10 minutes each side; the juices in the middle should run clear. Please note that this marinade was in contact with uncooked chicken, so always allow 5–10 minutes between the last time you baste and the end of cooking to ensure the marinade itself is thoroughly cooked.

★ Mix the lime juice, rum, soy sauce, and sugar in a bowl and add the pineapple wedges. Mix to coat thoroughly. Remove the wedges from the mixture, paint with a little groundnut (peanut) oil if you like, and place on the barbecue to char lightly and evenly.

★ Serve the chicken with the caramelized pineapple, salsa, and a rice salad.

FOR THIS RECIPE, WE NEED FIRST TO NECK A PINT OF MALIBU, THEN CLOSE OUR EYES AND IMAGINE OURSELVES ON THE SUNKISSED ISLAND OF JAMAICA, WHERE WE'RE GOING TO BE EATING SOME DELICIOUS JERK CHICKEN. KEEP IMAGINING, AND WATCH AS THE MEAT IS COOKED AND SMOKED OVER A FIRE OF PIMENTO WOOD, GIVING THE CHICKEN A VERY DISTINCTIVE TASTE. NOW OPEN YOUR EYES, DRINK SOME MORE MALIBU, GET UP OFF YOUR ASS, AND GO COOK THIS RECIPE.

CHARGRILLED STEAK FAJITAS
with chunky guacamole

2 long, thin pieces of bavette (skirt steak), about 6–7 oz. (175–200 g) each, or 12–14 oz. (350–400 g) bottom round (minute) steak

8 flour tortillas

romaine (cos) lettuce leaves

marinade

3 tablespoons freshly squeezed lime juice

1 garlic clove, crushed

1 teaspoon mild chili powder

3 tablespoons light olive oil

chunky guacamole

2 avocados, about 7 oz. (200 g) each

2 tablespoons freshly squeezed lime juice

4 scallions (spring onions), trimmed and thinly sliced

1 garlic clove, crushed

1 small fresh green chile pepper, seeded and thinly sliced (optional)

1 tablespoon olive oil

2–3 tomatoes, about 6 oz. (175 g), skinned, seeded, and chopped

3 tablespoons chopped fresh cilantro (coriander) leaves

sea salt

serves 4

TEX-MEX FOOD HAS SOMETHING OF A POOR REPUTATION, MAINLY BECAUSE EVERY MAN AND HIS DOG HAS JUMPED ON THE BANDWAGON AND IT'S OFTEN DONE INCREDIBLY BADLY. FORGET THE CRAPPY READY-MADE-FAJITA-DUST-IN-A-BOX-JUST-ADD-MEAT YOU BOUGHT FROM THE SUPERMARKET IN A MOMENT OF WEAKNESS. REGAIN SOME CULINARY DIGNITY BY MAKING THE REAL DEAL, AND THAT MEANS USING SKIRT STEAK (OR BAVETTE, AS IT'S ALSO KNOWN), FIRED ON THE GRILL. YOU CAN PICK UP THIS EXCELLENT CUT FROM ANY GOOD BUTCHER.

★ To make the marinade, put the lime juice, garlic, and chili powder in a shallow dish and whisk together. Gradually whisk in the olive oil. Put the steaks in the marinade and turn so that they are thoroughly coated. Cover and let marinate for 30 minutes while you prepare and light the grill/barbecue.

★ Meanwhile, to make the guacamole, scoop out the flesh from the avocados and put it in a bowl with the lime juice. Chop with a knife to give a chunky consistency. Add the scallions (spring onions), garlic, chile, if using, and olive oil and mix well. Add the tomatoes, cilantro (coriander), and salt, cover, and set aside.

★ When the flames have completely died down and ash is powdery white, pat the steak dry with paper towels (kitchen paper) and cook for about 1½ minutes each side. Set aside and let rest for 3–4 minutes while you warm the tortillas in a dry skillet or frying pan. Thinly slice the steak, then put a dollop of guacamole on each tortilla and top with slices of steak and shredded lettuce leaves. Carefully roll up the tortillas, press together, and cut in half diagonally.

KEFTA KEBABS WITH HARISSA COUSCOUS

THEY DEFINITELY KNOW THEIR STREET FOOD IN MOROCCO. THIS TIME IT'S GROUND (MINCED) LAMB OR BEEF (YOU HAVE A CHOICE) PIMPED UP WITH RAS-EL-HANOUT, MEANING "TOP OF THE SHOP." THIS RATHER LOVELY BLEND OF SPICES IS FOUND EVERYWHERE IN MOROCCO, AND EVERY SINGLE STALL OR VENDOR HAS THEIR OWN SUBTLE INTERPRETATION. IT'S FANTASTIC SERVED WITH HARISSA COUSCOUS, A VERY TYPICAL MOROCCAN ACCOMPANIMENT. FEEL FREE TO BANG IN SOME EXTRA HARISSA IF YOU LIKE IT FIERY.

kebabs

1 lb. (500 g) finely ground (minced) lean lamb or beef

1 onion, finely chopped

2 garlic cloves, crushed

1–2 teaspoons ground cinnamon

1–2 teaspoons Ras-el-Hanout

1 teaspoon sea salt

a small bunch of fresh flat leaf parsley, finely chopped

a small bunch of fresh cilantro (coriander), finely chopped

harissa couscous

1¼ cups (200 g) couscous

1 cup (240 ml) warm water

½ teaspoon sea salt

1 tablespoon olive oil

2–3 teaspoons Harissa (page 57)

2 tablespoons butter

serves 4–6

★ To make the kebabs, mix the meat with the other ingredients and knead well, lifting the mixture up and slapping it back into the bowl to knock out the air, until it is smooth and slightly sticky. Cover and chill in the refrigerator for about 1–2 hours to allow the flavors to mingle.

★ Meanwhile, prepare the couscous. Tip the couscous into a large bowl. Stir the salt into the water and pour it over the couscous, stirring all the time so that the water is absorbed evenly. Leave the couscous to swell for about 10 minutes, then, using your fingers, rub the oil and the harissa into the couscous.

★ Preheat the oven to 350°F (180°C) for the couscous and prepare the grill/barbecue for the kebabs. Divide the kebab mixture into 8–12 portions and mold them into fat sausage shapes. Insert a skewer through each one.

★ Tip the couscous into an ovenproof dish, dot the butter over the surface, and cover with a piece of foil or wet parchment paper. Put the dish in the preheated oven for 15 minutes, until the couscous is heated through. Place the kebabs on the grill and cook for 4–5 minutes on each side. Serve immediately.

TUSCAN-STYLE STEAK

YOU CAN'T GO FAR WRONG COOKING A WHOPPING GREAT STEAK. MAKE IT TUSCAN STYLE, MARINATED OVERNIGHT IN OLIVE OIL, GARLIC, AND ROSEMARY, AND YOU'RE PRETTY CLOSE TO PERFECTION. IN TUSCANY THE TRADITIONAL CUT TO USE IS KNOWN AS BISTECCA ALLA FIORENTINA, WHICH JUST ROLLS OFF THE TONGUE IN A PLEASING FASHION. YOU MIGHT WANT TO REMEMBER THAT AND DROP IT INTO CONVERSATION IF YOU WANT TO IMPRESS—POSSIBLY IN A FAUX ITALIAN ACCENT, IF YOU THINK YOU CAN MANAGE IT. ELSEWHERE IT'S CALLED A T-BONE, WHICH KIND OF SUCKS IN A RATHER FUNCTIONAL WAY.

1 large T-bone steak, about
1½ lb. (750 g) and cut to an even
thickness of 1–1¼ inches (3 cm)

6 tablespoons olive oil

2 garlic cloves, thinly sliced

3 sprigs of fresh rosemary

sea salt and freshly ground
black pepper

good-quality extra virgin olive oil,
for drizzling

to serve

sautéed potatoes

arugula (rocket) salad

lemon wedges (optional)

serves 2

★ Trim the excess fat off the edge of the steak, leaving a little if liked, and pat the steak dry with paper towels (kitchen paper). Pour the measured olive oil into a shallow dish and add the garlic and rosemary. Turn the steak in the oil, ensuring there is some garlic and rosemary on each side. Cover with a double layer of plastic wrap (clingfilm) and let marinate in the refrigerator for 24 hours, turning a couple of times. Bring back to room temperature before cooking it.

★ Prepare the grill/barbecue. Take the meat out of the marinade and remove any pieces of garlic or rosemary from the steak. Pat dry with paper towels. Put the steak on a rack about 3 inches (8 cm) above the coals and cook for about 4 minutes. Turn the steak over and cook for a further 3 minutes. (Cook for a couple minutes longer on each side for a medium-rare steak, although this dish is traditionally served rare.)

★ Transfer to a warm plate and season both sides with salt and pepper. Cover lightly with aluminum foil, then let rest for 5 minutes.

★ Stand the steak upright with the bone at the bottom and, using a sharp knife, remove the meat either side of the bone in one piece. Cut the meat into slices ¼–½ inch (1 cm) thick. Divide the slices between 2 serving plates. Pour over any meat juices that have accumulated under the meat and drizzle with the best extra virgin olive oil you can lay your hands on.

★ Serve with sautéed potatoes, an arugula (rocket) salad, and lemon wedges.

LAMB CUTLETS
with salsa salmoretta

GLANCE ACROSS AND LOOK AT THE INGREDIENTS OF SALSA SALMORETTA. HOW GOOD DOES THAT SOUND, EH? SHALLOT, TOMATO, GARLIC, CHILI, PARSLEY, AND OLIVE OIL—IMAGINE THAT LOT COMBINED IN A THOROUGHLY PLEASING FASHION AND ACCOMPANYING BARBECUED LAMB CUTLETS. WELL, THAT'S EXACTLY WHAT WILL HAPPEN IF YOU MAKE THIS RECIPE. OH YEAH. INCIDENTALLY, SALSA SALMORETTA IS FROM THE VALENCIA AND ALICANTE REGIONS OF SPAIN, SO I'M DEFINITELY GOING TO SAY WASH IT DOWN WITH A GLASS OR THREE OF ICE-COLD FINO SHERRY.

3 garlic cloves, crushed

2 teaspoons sweet Spanish paprika

4 sprigs of fresh thyme (leaves picked off 2 of them)

3 tablespoons olive oil

12 lamb cutlets, trimmed

sea salt and freshly ground black pepper

salsa salmoretta

1 large shallot, thinly sliced

3 ripe medium tomatoes

2 garlic cloves, finely chopped

1 dried hot red chili, seeded and finely chopped

1 tablespoon finely chopped, fresh flat leaf parsley

⅓ cup (90 ml) olive oil

1½ teaspoons red wine vinegar

sea salt and freshly ground black pepper

serves 4

★ To marinate the cutlets, put the garlic, paprika, thyme sprigs and leaves, olive oil, salt, and pepper in a flat dish and stir to mix. Add the cutlets, turn to coat, and let marinate for 2 hours or overnight.

★ Heat a grill/barbecue and cook over hot coals for 3 minutes on each side.

★ Meanwhile, to make the salsa salmoretta, put the shallot in a bowl and cover with cold water.

★ Cut a cross in the top of each tomato and put under a preheated hot broiler (grill) for 5 minutes, turning twice, until the skins are wrinkled and the flesh is soft. Peel, seed, and finely chop the flesh, then put in a bowl.

★ Meanwhile, crush the garlic, chili, and parsley to a paste with a mortar and pestle. Work in two-thirds of the chopped tomatoes. Drain the shallot and crush half of it with the tomatoes. Still stirring with the pestle, gradually add the oil to emulsify. Stir in the vinegar, the remaining tomatoes and shallot, salt, and pepper.

★ Serve the salsa with the cutlets.

SOUVLAKI IN PITA

LAST TIME I WAS IN GREECE, I STUFFED MYSELF SILLY WITH SOUVLAKI KEBABS. SERIOUSLY, I COULD NOT LEAVE THEM ALONE. I MUST HAVE EATEN ONE, MAYBE TWO EVERY DAY (YEAH, I'M A GREEDY BASTARDO). THEY ARE JUST SO BLOODY GOOD AND SO RIDICULOUSLY CHEAP. NOTHING YOU CAN BUY BACK HOME REALLY COMPARES, SO FOLLOW THIS RECIPE AND HAVE A GO AT MAKING YOUR OWN. THE TZATZIKI YOGURT, GARLIC, AND CUCUMBER DRESSING IS ABSOLUTELY ESSENTIAL, SO TOTALLY SMOTHER YOUR SOUVLAKI IN IT. OH, AND TRY TO GET GOOD-QUALITY PITA. NONE OF THAT DRY-AS-A-BONE, CHEAPO RUBBISH—TRUST ME AND MAKE IT GOOD.

4 large pita breads

water and olive oil, to moisten the bread

2 teaspoons chopped fresh oregano, or 1 teaspoon dried oregano, crushed

2 tablespoons freshly squeezed lemon juice

½ onion, coarsely grated

2 tablespoons extra virgin olive oil

1 lb. (500 g) lean pork or lamb (usually leg meat), cut into ¾-inch (2-cm) cubes

salad, such as

lettuce or cabbage, thinly sliced

cucumber, sliced

red bell pepper, sliced

tomatoes, cut into wedges

radishes, cut in half

red onion, sliced into rings

garlic dressing

½ cup (100 ml) plain yogurt, drained

4 garlic cloves, crushed

2 inches (5 cm) cucumber, coarsely grated, then squeezed dry

½ teaspoon sea salt

serves 4

★ Brush or sprinkle the pita breads all over with the water and oil and either broil (grill) or bake in a preheated oven at 350°F (180°C) for 3–5 minutes, or long enough to soften the bread, but not dry it. Cut off a strip from the long side, then pull open and part the sides of the breads to make a pocket. Push the strip inside. Keep the breads warm.

★ Prepare the grill/barbecue. Put the oregano, lemon juice, onion, and olive oil in a bowl and mash with a fork. Add the cubed meat and toss well. Cover and let marinate for 10–20 minutes. Drain, then thread the meat onto metal skewers. Cook on the preheated grill/barbecue for 5–8 minutes, or until golden outside and cooked through.

★ Put your choice of salad ingredients in a bowl, toss gently, then insert into the pockets of the pita breads.

★ To make the dressing, put the yogurt in a bowl, then beat in the garlic, cucumber, and salt. Add a large spoonful to each pocket.

★ Remove the hot, cooked meat from the skewers, then push it into the pockets. Serve immediately, while the meat and bread are hot and the salad still cool.

CHAPTER 4

SOMETHING FISHY

BARBECUE SHRIMP marinated in chile and soy

1 lb. (500 g) raw jumbo shrimp (tiger prawns), peeled but tails intact

8 oz. (250 g) cherry vine tomatoes

4 tablespoons olive oil

1 large green bell pepper, seeded and cut into 1¼-inch (3-cm) chunks

2 red jalapeño chile peppers, seeded and cut into ½-inch (1-cm) pieces

watercress and toasted pita bread, to serve

aïoli, to serve

marinade

1 garlic clove, crushed

1 fresh red chile pepper, seeded and finely chopped

1 tablespoon sesame oil

2 tablespoons dark soy sauce

grated zest and freshly squeezed juice of 1 unwaxed lime

2 tablespoons dark brown sugar

serves 4

* To make the marinade, mix together all the ingredients and blend to a smooth purée using a hand blender. If you don't have a hand blender, grind to a paste using a pestle and mortar.

* Put the shrimp (prawns) in a sealable food bag and pour in the marinade. Seal securely. Shake vigorously, and when all the shrimp look well coated, refrigerate, still in the bag, for about 2 hours.

* Put the tomatoes and half the olive oil in a small pan and gently warm for 5 minutes, or just long enough for the tomatoes to start to soften. Remove from the heat and let cool.

* Prepare the grill/barbecue. Take the shrimp out of the bag and place on a plate, reserving any remaining marinade. Thread the shrimp, tomatoes, pepper, and chiles onto 8 pre-soaked wooden skewers in a repeating sequence. Make sure you allow for enough of each ingredient on each skewer, and leave enough space at the ends of the skewers to handle when on the grill.

* In a small bowl, loosen the reserved marinade with 1–2 tablespoons of the remaining olive oil. Using a pastry brush, liberally coat the skewers with the marinade just before placing on the grill.

* Cook for a couple of minutes on each side until the shrimp turn pink and are cooked through. Serve with watercress, toasted pita bread, and a good dollop of aïoli.

EVERYONE LOVES BARBECUED SHRIMP OR PRAWNS. THEY TASTE AMAZING, AND, IMPORTANTLY FOR THE LAZY-ASS HOST WHO JUST WANTS TO RELAX WITH A DRINK AND EAT NICE GRUB, THEY TAKE PRACTICALLY NO TIME TO COOK, JUST A COUPLE MINUTES A SIDE. THIS RECIPE USES A REALLY QUICK-TO-THROW-TOGETHER ASIAN MARINADE, WHICH IS PARTICULARLY BANGING WITH SEAFOOD. MARINATING THE SHRIMP IN A BAG IS A GOOD WAY TO ENSURE THEY ALL GET A COATING OF SAUCE, AND IT SHOULD BE PRETTY MESS-FREE. SERVE WITH TOASTED PITA AND A DOLLOP OF GARLICKY AÏOLI. OH YES.

GRILLED SARDINE SANDWICHES
stuffed with chermoula

chermoula

2–3 garlic cloves, chopped

1 fresh red chile pepper, seeded and chopped

1 teaspoon sea salt

a small bunch each of fresh cilanto (coriander) and flat leaf parsley, chopped

2 teaspoons ground cumin

2 teaspoons paprika

4–5 tablespoons olive oil

freshly squeezed juice of 1 lemon

8 large or 16 small fresh sardines, gutted and boned with heads removed (you can ask the fishmonger to do this for you)

1 egg, beaten

sea salt

1 lemon, cut into quarters, to serve

serves 4

FRESH SARDINES ARE DIRT CHEAP AND TASTE FANTASTIC. WE'RE GOING TO GET THEM GUTTED AND BONED AND THEIR HEADS REMOVED (GET YOUR FISHMONGER TO DO IT, UNLESS YOU WANT TO GET MESSY AND DO IT YOURSELF), THEN SANDWICH A COUPLE TOGETHER WITH A FILLING OF THE CLASSIC MOROCCAN MARINADE FOR FISH, CHERMOULA, BEFORE FIRING THEM QUICKLY ON THE BARBECUE. A SQUEEZE OF LEMON OVER THE FINISHED ARTICLE WOULDN'T GO AMISS. I RECKON THESE WOULD ALSO BE TASTY IN A CRUSTY ROLL, MAYBE WITH A DIFFERENT FILLING—SALSA VERDE (PAGE 15) SPRINGS TO MIND. FEEL FREE TO PLAY AROUND AND EXPERIMENT.

★ Prepare the grill/barbecue. To make the chermoula, use a mortar and pestle to pound the garlic and chile with the salt to form a paste. Add the cilantro (coriander) and parsley leaves and pound to a coarse paste. Beat in the cumin and paprika and bind well with the olive oil and lemon juice (you can whizz all the ingredients together in an electric blender, if you prefer).

★ Open out the sardines and place half of them skin side down on a flat surface. Smear the chermoula over the sardines and brush the sides with beaten egg. Place the remaining butterflied sardines on top to sandwich the mixture together. Place them on the heated grill and cook for 2–3 minutes on each side. Sprinkle with salt and serve immediately with the lemon wedges to squeeze over them.

CHARGRILLED SHRIMP
with avocado chile salsa

SHRIMP (PRAWNS) AGAIN, PREFERABLY BIG ONES (YOU KNOW IT), BUT THIS TIME WE'RE GOING ALL
MEXICAN AND SERVING THEM WITH AN AVOCADO SALSA. YOU MAY THINK ALL AVOCADOS ARE EQUAL,
BUT THEY'RE NOT, OH NO. WHAT YOU WANT FOR THIS IS THE HASS AVOCADO, WHICH TASTES A BIT SPECIAL
COMPARED WITH YOUR STANDARD VARIETY. BEFORE YOU SERVE THE SALSA UP WITH YOUR SHRIMP,
HAVE A CHEEKY TASTE, ADJUST THE HEAT WITH MORE CHILE (I LIKE IT SPICY), AND CHECK THE SEASONING.

3–5 uncooked shrimp (prawns)
per person, depending on size,
with shells

2 tablespoons chili oil

freshly squeezed juice of 2 limes

a pinch of sea salt

2 tablespoons brown sugar

avocado chile salsa

2 red onions, quartered, then
finely sliced

1 fresh red chile pepper, such as
serrano, seeded and sliced
or diced

finely grated zest and freshly
squeezed juice of 1 unwaxed lime

2 large, ripe Hass avocados,
halved, with pits removed

2 ripe red tomatoes, halved,
seeded, and diced

a large handful of fresh cilantro
(coriander)

sea salt and coarsely ground
black pepper

serves 4

★ To make the salsa, put the onion, chile, and half the lime juice into a bowl
and set aside to marinate for a few minutes.

★ Using a small teaspoon or coffee spoon, scoop out small balls of
avocado into a serving bowl. Add the lime zest and remaining juice and
turn gently to coat.

★ Add the diced tomatoes to the onion mixture, toss gently, then add the
avocado. Tear the cilantro (coriander) leaves over the top and sprinkle with
the sea salt and black pepper.

★ Meanwhile, slit the shrimp (prawns) down the back and pull out the black
vein, if any. Put the chili oil, lime juice, salt, and sugar into a bowl, add the
shrimp, and toss to coat. Using your fingers, push the sauce into the slit and
set aside for 30 minutes. Prepare a medium–high grill/barbecue, add the
shrimp, then cook on both sides until just opaque.

★ Serve the shrimp with the avocado chile salsa. Flour tortillas, warmed on
the grill, are also a delicious accompaniment.

NOTE Always prepare avocado at the last moment and coat in a little citrus
juice. Avocado turns brown very quickly—don't believe the old wives' tale
that the pit prevents this.

GRILLED VINE-LEAF-WRAPPED SARDINES

IF I SAID THIS DISH MIGHT REMIND YOU OF VACATIONS IN GREECE, EATING IN WONDERFUL TAVERNAS, INDULGING IN LONG, LAZY LUNCHES WITH YOUR BARE FEET IN THE SAND, THE MIDDAY SUN BLAZING DOWN ONTO THE CANOPY ABOVE YOU, WHILE YOU SIPPED ICE-COLD RETSINA AND CONTEMPLATED A LAZY AFTERNOON SPENT SWIMMING IN THE SEA, YOU'D PROBABLY HAVE NO IDEA WHAT I WAS TALKING ABOUT. YOU WERE PROBABLY DRINKING CHEAP LIQUOR OUT OF PLASTIC BUCKETS OR SLEEPING OFF AN ALL-NIGHTER SPRAWLED ON A SUNBED WHILE YOUR "MATE" DREW A SUN-BLOCK PENIS ON YOUR BACK. BUT IF YOU WEREN'T, THIS RATHER LOVELY RECIPE'S FOR YOU.

black olive stuffing

1 cup (80 g) toasted bread crumbs

½ cup (60 g) cured black olives, pitted and chopped

a small bunch of fresh flat leaf parsley, roughly chopped

a small bunch of fresh oregano leaves

½ cup (120 ml) olive oil

sea salt and coarsely ground black pepper

12 sardines, gutted and cleaned

12 brined vine leaves

2 lemons, cut into thick slices

olive oil, to drizzle

serves 4

★ Put the bread crumbs, olives, parsley, and oregano in a bowl. Pour in the olive oil, a little at a time (you may not need it all), and stir until the stuffing begins to bind together. Season with salt and pepper.

★ With a sharp knife, cut along the bottom of the sardines where they have been gutted. Rinse them in cold water and pat dry with paper towels (kitchen paper).

★ Lay the vine leaves down on a work surface with the stem facing upward. Place a sardine on each leaf, then stuff each of the sardines with the Black Olive Stuffing. Fold the stem end of the leaf over the fish and tuck in both sides, then roll up.

★ Prepare a medium–high grill/barbecue. Grill the sardines for 5 minutes, then turn them over and grill for a further 5 minutes, until cooked. Lay the lemon slices on the grill and cook until charred.

★ Season the sardines and grilled lemons, and serve drizzled with olive oil.

GRILLED SARDINES
with salmoriglio sauce

12 fresh, fat sardines

olive oil, for brushing

lemon wedges, to serve

salmoriglio sauce

2 tablespoons red wine vinegar

1–2 teaspoons sugar

finely grated zest and freshly
squeezed juice of ½ unwaxed
lemon

4 tablespoons extra virgin olive oil

1 garlic clove, finely chopped

1 tablespoon crumbled
dried oregano

1 tablespoon salted capers,
rinsed and chopped

a grill rack

serves 4

WHEN I WAS YOUNGER, I WASN'T A FAN OF SARDINES. THE VERY IDEA THAT THEY WERE OILY FISH, AND THE CAT-FOOD SMELL OF THE CANNED VERSIONS MY PARENTS LIKED SO MUCH, KIND OF KILLED IT FOR ME. BUT NOW I'M OLDER, WISER, SOPHISTICATED, AND—I'M SURE MOST WOULD AGREE—EVEN MORE UNSPEAKABLY BEAUTIFUL (I DIGRESS), AND I NOW KNOW THAT IT'S ALL ABOUT FRESH SARDINES ON THE GRILL. THEY'RE SUPERB! OH, AND SO CHEAP, YEAH! APPARENTLY GREAT SHOALS OF SARDINES ARE TO BE FOUND IN MEDITERRANEAN WATERS IN MAY AND JUNE, SO UNLESS YOU WANT THEM TAKING OVER THE WORLD AND EVERY FACET OF HUMAN EXISTENCE AT SOME POINT IN THE NEAR FUTURE, IT'S YOUR DUTY TO EAT PLENTY.

★ To make the salmoriglio sauce, put the vinegar and sugar in a bowl and stir to dissolve. Add the lemon zest and juice. Beat in the olive oil, then add the garlic, oregano, and capers. Set aside to infuse.

★ Prepare a hot grill/barbecue. Using the back of a knife, scale the sardines, starting from the tail and working toward the head. Slit open the belly and remove the insides, then rinse the fish and pat dry. Clip off any fins you don't want to see. Brush the fish with olive oil and arrange on the grill rack.

★ Cook for about 3 minutes each side until sizzling hot and blackening. Serve with the salmoriglio spooned over the top, with lots of lemon wedges alongside.

HOT-SMOKED CREOLE SALMON

YEAH, YOU'VE CREMATED THE ODD BURGER AND SCORCHED A FEW SAUSAGES, SO YOU MAY THINK YOU'RE AN OLD HAND AT THE BARBECUE—A BIT OF A VETERAN. BUT STOP RIGHT THERE AND WIPE THAT SMUG LOOK OFF YOUR FACE. HAVE YOU REALLY BEEN USING YOUR BARBECUE TO ITS FULL POTENTIAL? I MEAN, HAVE YOU SMOKED FISH, FOR EXAMPLE? NO? WHAAAAT?! *FACE-SLAP* SMOKING FOOD IS ONE OF THE BEST THINGS EVER! IT'S OK, THOUGH, YOU MAY HAVE BEEN ALMOST CRIMINALLY NEGLIGENT, AND YOU PROBABLY DON'T DESERVE IT, BUT I'M GOING TO TELL YOU HOW TO GET SMOKING FISH AND YOU WILL BE INSTANTLY REBORN WITH THIS HOT-SMOKED CREOLE SALMON RECIPE. HALLELUJAH! (TOO MUCH, PERHAPS?)

4 salmon fillets, skinned, about 8 oz. (225 g) each

1 recipe Creole Rub (page 13)

a large handful of wood chips, such as hickory, soaked in cold water for 1 hour, drained

mango and sesame salsa

1 large ripe mango, peeled, pitted, and chopped

4 scallions (spring onions), chopped

1 hot fresh red chile, about 2 inches (5 cm) long, seeded and chopped

1 garlic clove, crushed

1 tablespoon light soy sauce

1 tablespoon lime juice

1 teaspoon sesame oil

½ tablespoon sugar

1 tablespoon chopped fresh cilantro (coriander)

sea salt and freshly ground black pepper

serves 4

★ Wash the salmon under cold running water and pat dry with paper towels (kitchen paper). Using tweezers, pull out any bones, then put the fish in a dish and work the Creole Rub all over it. Marinate in the refrigerator for at least 1 hour.

★ To make the salsa, put the chopped mango in a bowl, then add the scallions (spring onions), chile, garlic, soy sauce, lime juice, sesame oil, sugar, cilantro (coriander), salt, and pepper. Mix well and set aside for 30 minutes to let the flavors infuse.

★ Prepare a medium–high grill/barbecue. When the coals are ready, rake them into two piles and carefully place a drip tray in the middle. Tip half the soaked wood chips onto each pile of coals and cover with the lid, keeping any air vents open during cooking.

★ As soon as the wood chips start to smoke, put the salmon fillets in the center of the grill, cover, and cook for about 15–20 minutes or until the fish is cooked through.

★ To test the salmon, press it with your finger—the flesh should feel firm and start to open into flakes. Serve hot or cold, with the mango and sesame salsa.

SPICED RED SNAPPER
with chermoula

THERE'S SOMETHING EXTREMELY IMPRESSIVE ABOUT COOKING A WHOLE FISH OVER HOT COALS. WITHOUT SAYING A WORD, IT TELLS EVERYONE THAT YOU ARE HIGHLY CONFIDENT AND CAPABLE IN AN OUTDOOR ENVIRONMENT; THAT YOU CAN LOOK AFTER YOURSELF; THAT HUNTING AND NAVIGATING IN THE WILDERNESS, QUITE POSSIBLY WITH JUST THE STARS AS YOUR GUIDE, ARE NO PROBLEM AT ALL; THAT YOU CAN TIE KNOTS THAT ARE NOT JUST GRANNY KNOTS; AND THAT YOU CAN MAKE SHELTER AND BUILD FIRES WITH STICKS. YOU ARE A SURVIVALIST, AND NO MATTER WHAT HARDSHIP OR EXTREMES YOU MAY FACE, YOU'LL ENDURE THEM. YEAH, WHO CARES THAT YOU BOUGHT THAT RED SNAPPER FROM THE SUPERMARKET FISH COUNTER AND THAT YOU ALMOST GOT LOST ON THE WAY THERE.

★ Wash the snapper in cold water and pat dry. Lay the fish on a platter big enough to hold them all.

★ Stuff the snapper with the sliced lemons and brush the fish inside and out with the chermoula. Season with salt and pepper.

★ Prepare a medium–high grill/barbecue. Lay the fish on the hot grill and cook for 8–10 minutes on each side, depending on the thickness of the fish, until the flesh is cooked through. Remove the fish, cover with foil, and let rest for 5 minutes.

★ Serve the fish with the lemon and lime quarters.

4 red snapper (about 12 oz./350 g each), cleaned and well scaled

2 lemons, thinly sliced

1 recipe of chermoula (page 68)

sea salt and coarsely ground black pepper

2 lemons, quartered, to serve

2 limes, quartered, to serve

serves 4

GRILLED LOBSTERS
with two butters

FORGET SHRIMP, FORGET MASSIVE PRAWNS, FORGET THE WHOLE CAST OF "FINDING NEMO"—THE ABSOLUTE PINNACLE OF AQUATIC STUFFING-YOUR-FACE-LUXURY HAS TO BE LOBSTER. IT REALLY HAS NO EQUAL. YEAH, IT CAN BE FIDDLY DIGGING AROUND IN THE SHELL AND CRACKING THE CLAWS TO GET AT THE GORGEOUS MEAT INSIDE, BUT THAT'S PART OF THE CHARM. YOU HAVE TO WORK A BIT TO GET THE GOOD STUFF. OF COURSE, YOU MUST BE PREPARED TO GET ALL MEDIEVAL, AND BY THIS I MEAN BOILING YOUR LOBSTER ALIVE, THEN CUTTING IT IN HALF AND FINISHING IT OVER A FLAMING GRILL. UNLUCKY FOR THE LOBSTER, BUT IT CAN TAKE SOLACE IN THE FACT THAT IT'LL TASTE AMAZING SMOTHERED IN THE FLAVORED BUTTER. SEEING AS YOU'RE BEING ALL EXTRAVAGANT AND THAT, I SUGGEST GOING BALLS-TO-THE-WALL AND WASHING THE LOBSTER DOWN WITH ICE-COLD CHAMPAGNE.

2 teaspoons sea salt

4 lobsters (about 1½–2 lb./ 750–900 g each)

Saffron Butter (page 19)

sea salt and coarsely ground black pepper

4 lemons, cut into quarters, to serve

serves 4

★ Fill a large stock or pasta pot three quarters full with water and add the salt. Bring to a boil and carefully add 2 of the lobsters. Cook for 10 minutes, then remove and place on a wooden cutting board. Cook the remaining 2 lobsters in the same way.

★ When the lobsters are cool enough to handle, cut them in half from head to tail using a sharp knife or kitchen scissors. Season well with salt and pepper.

★ Lay the lobster halves, cut side down, on a medium–high grill/barbecue and cook for 2–3 minutes. Turn them over and dot with the flavored butter. Continue to cook for a further 3–4 minutes, until the butter has melted.

★ Serve immediately with more butter, lemons, and ice-cold Champagne.

GRILLED TUNA STEAKS
with peperonata

PRETTY MUCH EVERYONE SEEMS TO LIKE TUNA, PROBABLY BECAUSE IT'S THE LEAST "FISHY"-TASTING EDIBLE CITIZEN OF THE AQUATIC WORLD. IT'S A VERY RICH MEAT, THOUGH, AND IN ITALY, WHERE THIS RECIPE ORIGINATES AND WHERE THEY KNOW A THING OR TWO ABOUT COOKING, IT'S ALWAYS CUT THINLY. HOW DOES MARINATING YOUR THIN FISH IN MUSTARD AND BOOZE (IN THE FORM OF GRAPPA) SOUND? YEAH! IT GIVES THE TUNA STEAKS A PIQUANT CRUST THAT GOES REALLY WELL WITH THE PEPERONATA, WHICH IS A CRACKING MEDITERRANEAN STEW OF ONIONS, TOMATOES, AND BELL PEPPERS.

4 tuna loin steaks cut ½ inch (1 cm) thick

olive oil, for cooking

sea salt and freshly ground black pepper

marinade

4 garlic cloves

3 tablespoons Dijon mustard

2 tablespoons grappa or brandy

peperonata

6 tablespoons olive oil

2 lb. (1 kg) fresh ripe tomatoes, peeled, seeded, and chopped, or two 14-oz. (400-g) cans chopped tomatoes

½ teaspoon hot red pepper (dried red chili) flakes

2 medium onions, thinly sliced

3 garlic cloves, chopped

3 red bell peppers, cut into strips

serves 4

★ To make the marinade, crush the garlic, put it in a bowl, and beat in the mustard and grappa. Season with salt and pepper and spread over the cut sides of the tuna. Arrange in a non-metal dish, cover, and let marinate in a cool place for about 1 hour.

★ To make the peperonata, heat 3 tablespoons of the oil in a pan, then add the tomatoes and pepper (chili) flakes. Cook over medium heat for 10 minutes, or until the tomatoes disintegrate.

★ Heat the remaining oil in a skillet or frying pan, add the onions, garlic, and peppers, and sauté for about 10 minutes until beginning to soften. Add the pepper mixture to the tomatoes and simmer, covered, for 45 minutes, until very soft. Taste and season with salt and pepper.

★ Preheat the grill/barbecue. Sprinkle the steaks with olive oil and grill for 1–2 minutes on each side, until crusty on the outside but still pink in the middle. Serve with the peperonata, which can be served hot or cold.

SALT-CRUSTED SHRIMP
with tomato, avocado, and olive salad

COOKING SEAFOOD ENCRUSTED IN SALT IS AN INTERESTING TECHNIQUE, WHICH—BELIEVE IT OR NOT—PROTECTS THE FLESH SO THAT IT STAYS MOIST. INCREDIBLY, CONSIDERING YOU'RE SMOTHERING THE WHOLE LOT IN SALT, THE FINISHED ARTICLE DOESN'T TASTE SALTY, SO DON'T PANIC. AS ALWAYS WHEN IT COMES TO SHRIMP, PRAWNS, OR VARIOUS OTHER THINGS YOU'LL ENCOUNTER THROUGHOUT YOUR LIFE, BIG WHOPPERS ARE ALWAYS BETTER. IF AT SOME POINT IN THE FUTURE YOU FIND YOURSELF CHEWING ON A SHRIMP AS BIG AS A BABY'S ARM, YOU'LL KNOW YOU'VE MADE IT *CRUSTACEAN-HIGH-FIVE*.

20 large uncooked
shell-on shrimp (prawns)

1 tablespoon extra virgin olive oil

3 tablespoons sea salt

tomato, avocado, and olive salad

4–6 large ripe tomatoes, sliced

1 large ripe avocado, cut in half,
pitted, and sliced

2 oz. (50 g) black olives, pitted

a handful of fresh mint leaves

4 tablespoons extra virgin olive oil

1 tablespoon reduced balsamic
vinegar*

shavings of fresh Parmesan cheese

sea salt and freshly ground
black pepper

serves 4

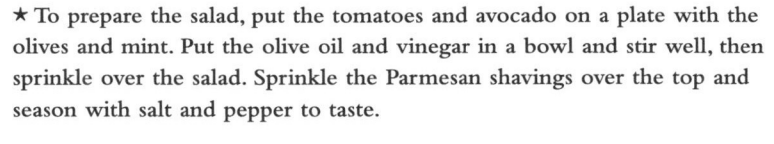

★ To prepare the salad, put the tomatoes and avocado on a plate with the olives and mint. Put the olive oil and vinegar in a bowl and stir well, then sprinkle over the salad. Sprinkle the Parmesan shavings over the top and season with salt and pepper to taste.

★ Using kitchen shears/scissors, cut down the back of each shrimp (prawn) to reveal the intestinal vein. Pull it out and discard, but leave the shell on. Wash the shrimp under cold running water, pat dry with paper towels (kitchen paper), and put in a bowl. Sprinkle over the olive oil and toss well. Put the salt on a plate and use to coat the shrimp.

★ Preheat the grill/barbecue, then cook the shrimp over hot coals for 2–3 minutes on each side, until cooked through. Let cool slightly, peel off the shells, then serve with the tomato, avocado, and olive salad.

NOTE To reduce the balsamic vinegar, put 1¼ cups (300 ml) in a saucepan and boil gently until it has reduced by about two-thirds. Let cool.

SEARED SWORDFISH
with new potatoes, beans, and olives

HERE'S AN IMPORTANT POINT TO REMEMBER WHEN COOKING FISH: YOU CAN ALWAYS THROW IT BACK ON THE GRILL FOR A BIT IF IT'S UNDERCOOKED, BUT ONCE YOU'VE TURNED IT INTO SHOE LEATHER, THERE'S NO GOING BACK. SOME FISH IS MORE FORGIVING THAN OTHERS, BUT SWORDFISH IS EASY TO OVERCOOK, SO WATCH HOW YOU GO. THE ACCOMPANIMENT OF NEW POTATOES, BEANS, AND OLIVES WITH A LEMONY DRESSING IS AN ABSOLUTE CLASSIC FOR ANY WHITE FISH, SO STORE THE IDEA AWAY UP THERE *TAPS HEAD* FOR FUTURE USE.

4 swordfish steaks, about 8 oz. (225 g) each

1 tablespoon extra virgin olive oil

1 lb. (500 g) new potatoes, halved if large

8 oz. (225 g) string beans, trimmed

⅓ cup (60 g) pitted black or green olives, chopped

balsamic vinegar, to serve

dressing

6 tablespoons extra virgin olive oil

2 tablespoons freshly squeezed lemon juice

½ teaspoon sugar

1 tablespoon chopped fresh chives

sea salt and freshly ground black pepper

serves 4

★ Brush the swordfish steaks with the oil, season with salt and pepper, and set aside.

★ To make the dressing, put the oil into a bowl and add the lemon juice, sugar, chives, salt, and pepper. Beat well and set aside.

★ Cook the potatoes in a pan of lightly salted boiling water for 10 minutes, then add the beans and cook for a further 3–4 minutes, or until the potatoes and beans are just tender. Drain well, add the olives and half the dressing, and toss well.

★ Cook the swordfish steaks on a preheated grill/barbecue for about 1½ minutes on each side. Let rest in a warm oven for 5 minutes, then serve with the warm potato salad, sprinkled with the remaining dressing and a splash of balsamic vinegar.

SICILIAN-SPICED SEABASS

AS I'VE MENTIONED PREVIOUSLY, A WHOLE FISH COOKED ON THE BARBECUE IS INCREDIBLY IMPRESSIVE. SERVE IT ON A PLATTER AND LET PEOPLE HELP THEMSELVES, FAMILY-STYLE. HERE WE'RE COOKING SEABASS RUBBED WITH SICILIAN SPICES, ACCOMPANIED WITH CHARGRILLED TOMATOES AND BABY FENNEL. IF A WHOLE FISH DOESN'T APPEAL (WHAAAT?), YOU COULD USE THE SAME SICILIAN RUB AND ACCOMPANYING VEGETABLES WITH TUNA OR SWORDFISH STEAKS. BUT IF YOU REALLY WANT TO IMPRESS, A WHOLE RACEHORSE'S HEAD WILL DEFINITELY MAKE PEOPLE SIT UP AND TAKE NOTICE. (IF YOU HAVEN'T SEEN "THE GODFATHER," THAT REFERENCE WILL MEAN NOTHING.)

1 rounded teaspoon fennel seeds

1 rounded teaspoon dried oregano

1 teaspoon cumin seeds

1 teaspoon sea salt

1 teaspoon green or black peppercorns

¼ teaspoon dried hot red pepper (chili) flakes

6 small seabass, gutted and scaled (ask the fishmonger or assistant at the fish counter to do this for you)

extra virgin olive oil spray

3 unwaxed lemons

a few bay leaves

4 baby fennel bulbs

12 oz. (350 g) cherry tomatoes

wedges of lemon, to serve

serves 6

★ Prepare a medium–high grill/barbecue.

★ Crush the fennel seeds, oregano, cumin seeds, salt, peppercorns, and pepper (chili) flakes together thoroughly in a mortar with a pestle. Make 3 slashes in each side of each fish with a sharp knife. Spray the fish with olive oil and rub the pounded spices over the fish and into the slits. Cut 2 of the lemons in half vertically, then cut 1½ into thin slices. Cut or tear the bay leaves into halves or thirds. Place half a slice of lemon and a piece of bay leaf in each slit.

★ Cut each fennel bulb into quarters lengthwise and thread the cherry tomatoes onto pre-soaked wooden skewers. Spray the fish, fennel, and tomatoes with oil and grill until charred, turning them halfway through. Serve immediately, with lemon wedges.

SHRIMP A LA PLANCHA

ENORMOUS SHRIMP (PRAWNS) WITH A SIMPLE, TANGY SALSA. DOES IT GET ANY BETTER? TO AVOID DISAPPOINTMENT, YOU REALLY MUST GET THE FRESHEST SHRIMP YOU CAN LAY YOUR HANDS ON, AND MAKE SURE THEY ARE ABSOLUTELY WHOPPING BEASTS. YEAH, THEY'LL BE COSTLY, BUT LIFE'S FOR LIVING AND NOTHING SAYS YOU'RE LIVING LIFE MORE THAN INDULGING IN SOME GIANT SHRIMP ACTION. OH, AND PUT ASIDE ANY DIGNITY YOU MAY HAVE: SUCK AND CRUNCH THE SHELLS TO GET ALL THE SAUCE OUT. BUT DON'T ACTUALLY EAT THE SHELLS ... THAT WOULD BE STUPID.

2 tomatoes

1 tablespoon very finely chopped onion

1 fresh green chile pepper

a small bunch of fresh cilantro (coriander), finely chopped

¼ teaspoon sea salt

1½ tablespoons butter

6 large shrimp (prawns), shell on

5 garlic cloves, very finely chopped

serves 2

★ Prepare a medium–high grill/barbecue.

★ Put the tomatoes, onion, chile, and 2 cups (500 ml) water in a pan over high heat. Cover with a lid and bring to a boil, then turn the heat down to low and simmer for about 5–7 minutes.

★ Drain, then allow to cool for at least 5 minutes before transferring to a food processor with the cilantro (coriander) and half the salt. Whizz for 2 minutes and set aside.

★ Put the shrimp (prawns) on the grill, with a little bit of butter on each, and cook for 3–4 minutes or until opaque and cooked through, turning occasionally. Add the garlic and cook for 2 minutes.

★ Divide the shrimp between 2 dishes and spoon some of the cilantro sauce over them. Serve with the remaining sauce on the side for dipping.

BARBECUED FISH

bathed in oregano and lemon

THE TITLE OF THIS RECIPE SOUNDS RATHER GENERIC, BUT IT'S INCREDIBLY USEFUL TO KNOW THAT BASICALLY
CHARGRILLING ALMOST ANY WHOLE FISH WITH LEMON, OREGANO, AND GARLIC IN THIS WAY WILL ACHIEVE
REALLY NICE RESULTS. NO FUSS, NO FAFF. THIS WILL WORK PERFECTLY WELL WITH BREAM, SNAPPER, RED
MULLET, OR EVEN TROUT. SO IT'S GREAT FOR WHEN YOU TURN UP AT THE FISHMONGER WITH A SPECIFIC FISH
IN MIND AND, INEXPLICABLY, THEY DON'T HAVE IT. YOU'LL NEVER BE FLUMMOXED AGAIN!

2 unwaxed lemons

1 cup (250 ml) extra virgin
olive oil

1 tablespoon dried oregano

2 garlic cloves, finely chopped

2 tablespoons chopped fresh
flat leaf parsley

6 bream, snapper, red mullet, or
trout (about 12 oz./350 g each),
well cleaned and scaled

sea salt and freshly ground
black pepper

serves 6

★ Grate the zest of 1 lemon into a small bowl and squeeze in the juice. Add
¾ cup (225 ml) of the oil, the oregano, garlic, parsley, salt, and pepper. Leave
to infuse for at least 1 hour.

★ Wash and dry the fish inside and out. Using a sharp knife, cut several
slashes into each side. Squeeze the juice from the remaining lemon into a
bowl, add the remaining ¼ cup (25 ml) of oil, salt, and pepper, and rub the
mixture all over the fish.

★ Heat the flat plate of an
outdoor grill/barbecue for
10 minutes, add the fish, and
cook for 3–4 minutes on each
side until charred and cooked
through. Alternatively, use a
large, heavy skillet, frying pan,
or stove-top grill pan. Transfer
the fish to a large, warm platter,
pour over the lemon dressing,
and let rest for 5 minutes
before serving.

RED SNAPPER
with parsley salad

RED SNAPPER HAS WHITE, SWEET, FIRM FLESH AND TASTES FANTASTIC WHEN GRILLED LIKE THIS, WHOLE. THE PARSLEY SALAD IS A BIT GOOD TOO. PEOPLE DON'T OFTEN THINK OF USING FLAT LEAF PARSLEY AS THE MAIN COMPONENT OF A SALAD, BUT IT WORKS REALLY WELL. THE VERJUICE IN THE DRESSING IS AN INTERESTING INGREDIENT, MADE FROM THE JUICE OF UNRIPE GREEN GRAPES. IT'S BEEN KNOCKING AROUND FOREVER—THE ROMANS LOVED IT. THE TASTE IS ACIDIC, BUT NOT AS TART AS VINEGAR, SO IT'S GREAT IN SALAD DRESSINGS.

4 red snapper (about 12 oz./350 g each), cleaned and well scaled

1 recipe Herb, Lemon, and Garlic Marinade (page 11)

parsley salad

⅓ cup (50 g) raisins

2 tablespoons verjuice or white grape juice*

leaves from a large bunch of fresh flat leaf parsley

scant ¼ cup (25 g) pine nuts, toasted

2 oz. (50 g) feta cheese, crumbled

3 tablespoons extra virgin olive oil

2 teaspoons balsamic vinegar

sea salt and freshly ground black pepper

serves 4

★ Using a sharp knife, cut several slashes into each side of the fish. Put into a shallow ceramic dish and add the marinade. Let marinate in the refrigerator for 4 hours, but return to room temperature for 1 hour before cooking.

★ Just before cooking the fish, make the salad. Put the raisins into a bowl, add the verjuice, and let soak for 15 minutes. Drain and set the liquid aside. Put the parsley, pine nuts, soaked raisins, and feta into a bowl. Put the olive oil, vinegar, and reserved raisin liquid into a separate bowl and mix well. Pour over the salad and toss until the leaves are well coated. Season with salt and pepper.

★ Prepare the grill/barbecue, then cook the fish over hot coals for 4–5 minutes on each side. Let rest briefly, and serve with the salad.

NOTE Verjuice is available from Italian gourmet stores. If you can't find it, use white grape juice instead.

VINE-WRAPPED MONKFISH KEBABS
with herb sauce

about 30 preserved vine leaves

4–5 large, skinless fillets of white fish, with all bones removed

marinade

2–3 garlic cloves, crushed

1–2 teaspoons ground cumin

4 tablespoons olive oil

freshly squeezed juice of 1 lemon

1 teaspoon sea salt

tangy herb sauce

¼ cup (60 ml) white wine vinegar or freshly squeezed lemon juice

1–2 tablespoons sugar

a pinch of saffron threads

1 onion, finely chopped

2 garlic cloves, finely chopped

2–3 scallions (spring onions), finely sliced

a thumb-sized piece of fresh ginger, peeled and grated

2 fresh hot red or green chile peppers, finely sliced

a small bunch of fresh cilantro (coriander), finely chopped

a small bunch of fresh mint, finely chopped

sea salt

serves 4

RIGHT AT THE START I'M GOING TO SAY THIS: DON'T LIKE MONKFISH? DON'T WORRY. YOU CAN MAKE THESE VINE-WRAPPED KEBABS WITH PRETTY MUCH ANY WHITE FISH. NO PROBLEM AT ALL, GO CRAZY, BUT—JUST FOR THE RECORD—HADDOCK WORKS WELL. THE BEAUTY OF WRAPPING YOUR FISH FILLETS IN VINE LEAVES, APART FROM LOOKING ALL MEDITERRANEAN AND SOPHISTICATED, IS THAT THE LEAVES CRISP UP WHILE THE FISH IS COOKING AWAY, AND THEY KEEP THE FLESH MOIST. BELIEVE ME, THAT'S EXACTLY WHAT YOU WANT.

★ Wash the vine leaves and soak them in several changes of water for 1 hour.

★ To prepare the marinade, mix all the ingredients in a shallow bowl. Cut each fish fillet into roughly 8 bite-size pieces and coat in the marinade. Cover and let chill in the refrigerator for 1 hour.

★ Meanwhile, prepare the tangy herb sauce. Put the vinegar in a small pan with the sugar and 1–2 tablespoons water. Heat until the sugar has dissolved. Bring to a boil for 1 minute, then leave to cool. Add the other ingredients, mix well, and spoon the sauce into small individual bowls.

★ Lay the prepared vine leaves on a flat surface and place a piece of marinated fish in the center of each one. Fold the edges over the fish and wrap the leaf up into a small package. Push the packages carefully onto pre-soaked wooden skewers and brush the leaves with any remaining marinade.

★ Prepare the grill/barbecue. Cook the kebabs for 2–3 minutes on each side. Serve immediately, with a dish of the tangy herb sauce on the side for dipping.

SCALLOPS
with lemongrass and butter

SCALLOPS TASTE ABSOLUTELY GORGEOUS, AND BY VIRTUE OF THE FLAT SHELL, THEY BASICALLY COME WITH THEIR OWN COMBINED COOKING VESSEL AND SERVING PLATTER. IF YOU'RE DOING THIS THE HARD WAY, YOU'VE GOT YOUR HANDS ON LIVE SCALLOPS AND YOU'LL BE OPENING AND CLEANING THEM YOURSELF. IT'S MESSY, BUT THESE WILL BE THE FRESHEST, BEST-TASTING SCALLOPS GOING. MORE LIKELY, YOUR FISHMONGER WILL HAVE SUPPLIED THE SCALLOPS AND DONE THE HARD WORK FOR YOU. THEY WON'T BE QUITE AS NICE, BUT THEY'RE STILL LOVELY. THE POINT IS THAT YOU MIGHT NOT HAVE THE SHELLS. IF SO, YOU CAN THREAD THE SCALLOPS ONTO SKEWERS, BRUSH THEM WITH THE MELTED BUTTER MIXTURE, AND GRILL FOR A MINUTE ON EACH SIDE. BUT BELIEVE ME, YOU REALLY WANT TO COOK 'EM IN THE SHELLS.

2 lemongrass stalks

grated zest and juice of ½ large unwaxed lime

1 stick (125 g) butter, softened

1 red bird's eye chile pepper, seeded and finely chopped

1 tablespoon Thai fish sauce

24 large sea scallops

24 scallop shells

1 tablespoon chopped fresh cilantro (coriander)

freshly ground black pepper

serves 4

★ Using a sharp knife, trim the lemongrass stalks to about 6 inches (15 cm), then remove and discard the tough outer leaves. Chop the inner stalk very thinly and put in a pan with the lime zest and juice, butter, chile, and fish sauce. Heat gently until the butter has melted, then simmer for 1 minute. Remove the pan from the heat and let cool.

★ Remove and discard the corals from the scallops and cut through to detach the meat from the shell. Put the scallops back on the shells and spoon a little of the butter mixture over each one.

★ Preheat the grill/barbecue, then put the shells on the grill rack and cook for 3–4 minutes, turning the scallops over halfway through with tongs. Serve immediately, sprinkled with chopped cilantro (coriander) and freshly ground black pepper.

DUKKAH-CRUSTED TUNA
with preserved lemon salsa

IN THE MIDDLE EAST, DUKKAH—A MIX OF CRUSHED NUTS AND SPICES—IS SERVED AS A SIDE DISH FOR DIPPING WARM, OLIVE OIL-DRIZZLED BREAD INTO. NICE. HOWEVER, IT'S ALSO RATHER GOOD USED AS A COATING FOR FISH, IN THIS CASE CHARGRILLED TUNA. ANY LEFTOVER DUKKAH KEEPS FOR AGES IN A SEALED PLASTIC CONTAINER. YOU CAN USE IT FOR ALL SORTS: TOSS IT THROUGH A SALAD, OR USE IT IN PLACE OF BREAD CRUMBS TO COAT MEAT, EGGS, OR ANYTHING SAVORY, REALLY. YOU CAN PICK UP PRESERVED LEMONS EVERYWHERE NOWADAYS; PRETTY MUCH ALL SUPERMARKETS STOCK THEM IN LITTLE JARS.

4 tuna steaks, about 8 oz. (225 g) each

3 tablespoons sesame seeds

2 tablespoons coriander seeds

½ tablespoon cumin seeds

¼ cup blanched almonds, chopped

½ teaspoon salt

freshly ground black pepper

olive oil, for brushing

preserved lemon salsa

1 preserved lemon

¼ cup (25 g) semi-dried tomatoes

2 scallions (spring onions), very finely chopped

1 tablespoon coarsely chopped fresh flat leaf parsley

3 tablespoons extra virgin olive oil

¼ teaspoon sugar

serves 4

★ To make the salsa, chop the preserved lemon and tomatoes finely and put into a bowl. Stir in the scallions (spring onions), parsley, olive oil, and sugar and set aside until ready to serve.

★ Wash the tuna steaks under cold running water and pat dry with paper towels (kitchen paper).

★ Put the sesame seeds into a dry skillet or frying pan and toast over medium heat until golden and aromatic. Remove and let cool. Repeat with the coriander seeds, cumin seeds, and almonds. Transfer to a spice grinder (or clean coffee grinder) and grind. Alternatively, use a mortar and pestle. Add the salt and a little pepper.

★ Preheat the grill/barbecue. Brush the tuna steaks with olive oil and coat with the dukkah mixture. Cook over hot coals for 1 minute on each side, top with the salsa, and serve.

CLAM PACKAGE with garlic butter

2 lb. (1 kg) littleneck (vongole) clams

1 stick (125 g) unsalted butter, softened

grated zest and freshly squeezed juice of ½ unwaxed lemon

2 garlic cloves, crushed

2 tablespoons chopped fresh flat leaf parsley

freshly ground black pepper

fresh crusty bread, to serve

serves 4

CLAMS ON THE GRILL ARE EASY TO DO, INEXPENSIVE, AND TASTY, AND MAKE YOU IRRESISTIBLE TO ANYONE WITHIN A 10-FOOT RADIUS. TRUE.

★ Wash the clams in cold running water and scrub the shells. Discard any with broken shells or any that refuse to close when tapped lightly with a knife. Shake the clams dry and divide between 4 pieces of foil.

★ Put the butter, lemon zest and juice, garlic, parsley, and pepper into a bowl and beat well. Divide equally between the clams. Wrap the foil over the clams and seal the edges to form packages.

★ Prepare the grill/barbecue, then put the packages onto the grill rack and cook for 5 minutes. Check one parcel to see if the clams have opened, and serve if ready or cook a little longer if needed. Serve with crusty bread.

SQUID PIRI-PIRI

8 medium squid bodies, about 8 oz. (225 g) each

freshly squeezed juice of 1 lemon, plus extra lemon wedges, to serve

sea salt

piri-piri sauce

8 small fresh red chile peppers

1¼ cups (300 ml) extra virgin olive oil

1 tablespoon white wine vinegar

sea salt and freshly ground black pepper

serves 4

I'LL TELL YOU A SECRET: HOT CHILE PIRI-PIRI TASTES SO GOOD WITH GRILLED CHICKEN THAT I'M GOING TO SET UP A RESTAURANT SPECIALIZING IN BIRDS SMOTHERED IN THE STUFF. I'LL BE FILTHY RICH! EH? WHAT'S THAT? SHIT. YEAH, IT GOES REALLY WELL WITH SQUID TOO.

★ To prepare the squid, put the squid body on a board, cut down one side and open the tube out flat. Scrape away any remaining insides, wash and dry well.

★ Skewer each opened-out tube with 2 pre-soaked wooden skewers, running them up the long sides of each piece. Rub a little sea salt over each one and squeeze over the lemon juice. Marinate in the refrigerator for 30 minutes.

★ Meanwhile, to make the piri-piri, finely chop the whole chiles without seeding them and transfer to a small jar or bottle. Add the oil, vinegar, and a little salt and pepper. Shake well and set aside.

★ Prepare a hot grill/barbecue. Baste the squid with a little piri-piri and cook for 1–1½ minutes on each side, until charred. Drizzle with extra sauce and serve with lemon wedges.

PEPPER 'N' SPICE CHICKEN

TAKING INSPIRATION FROM THE RATHER SUPERB ASIAN CLASSIC SALT 'N' PEPPER SQUID, WE HAVE THE RATHER CRACKING PEPPER 'N' SPICE CHICKEN. LET'S CONSIDER THIS FOR A MOMENT. OF COURSE, ON THE DOWNSIDE, A CHICKEN OBVIOUSLY HAS A HELL OF A LOT FEWER LEGS THAN A SQUID, BUT TURN THAT FROWN UPSIDE DOWN, PEOPLE: DESPITE BEING A LOSER TO SQUID IN THE LIMB DEPARTMENT, A CHICKEN BOASTS MEATY, CHUNKY LEGS. IN ADDITION, A SQUID IS KIND OF UGLY AND A CHICKEN IS KIND OF CUTE ... AND AS WE ALL KNOW, CUTE MAKES BETTER EATING. SO FOR BEST RESULTS, MAKE THIS RECIPE USING THE MOST ATTRACTIVE CHICKEN YOU CAN FIND.

1 small chicken

1 recipe Asian Rub (page 13)

2 tablespoons toasted sesame oil

1–2 limes, cut into wedges

Sweet Chile Sauce (page 21), to serve

serves 4

* Cut the chicken into 12 pieces and put them in a dish. Add the rub and sesame oil and work well into the chicken pieces. Let marinate in the refrigerator for 2 hours, but return to room temperature for 1 hour before cooking.

* Prepare a medium–high grill/barbecue. Cook the chicken for 15–20 minutes, turning after 10 minutes, until it is cooked through and the juices run clear when the thickest part of the meat is pierced with a skewer. Squeeze lime juice over, let cool slightly, and serve with the Sweet Chile Sauce.

WHOLE CHICKEN
roasted on the barbecue

WHACKING A WHOLE CHICKEN ON THE BARBECUE IS A CAPITAL IDEA. I BLOODY LOVE IT. IN FACT, I RECKON I COULD EAT ONE OF THESE ALL BY MYSELF. IF YOU'RE AN EQUALLY GREEDY B*STARD, THROW ANOTHER ONE ON FOR EVERYONE ELSE TO SHARE. USE THE BEST CHICKEN YOU CAN FIND, PREFERABLY FREE RANGE AND ORGANIC. YEAH, IT'S MORE EXPENSIVE, BUT IT TASTES MUCH BETTER, AND I KNOW IT'S A BIT RICH TO SAY SO CONSIDERING YOU'RE EATING THE POOR BUGGER, BUT THE LIFE THEY LEAD BEFORE *FINGER ACROSS THROAT, TONGUE POKING OUT* IS THAT MUCH NICER. FOR THIS RECIPE YOU NEED A BARBECUE WITH A LID. IF YOU DON'T HAVE ONE, DON'T FREAK OUT, JUST CUT THE CHICKEN IN HALF AND COOK IT ON THE GRILL FOR 15 MINUTES PER SIDE. SERVE WITH A GREEN SALAD AND MAYBE SOME CRÈME FRAÎCHE SPIKED WITH CHOPPED TARRAGON.

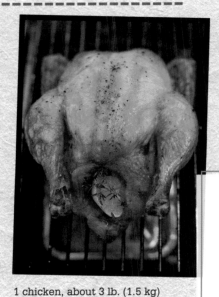

1 chicken, about 3 lb. (1.5 kg)

1 lemon, halved

4 garlic cloves, peeled

a small bunch of fresh thyme

extra virgin olive oil

sea salt and freshly ground black pepper

serves 4–6

★ Pat the chicken dry with paper towels (kitchen paper) and rub all over with the halved lemon. Put the lemon halves inside the body cavity with the garlic, cloves, and thyme. Rub a little olive oil into the skin and season liberally with salt and pepper.

★ Prepare a medium–high grill/barbecue. When the coals are ready, rake them into two piles and carefully place a drip tray in the middle. Remove the grill rack and brush or spray it with oil. Return it to the grill and put the chicken on the rack above the drip tray. Cover with the lid, then cook for 1 hour or until the skin is golden, the flesh is cooked through, and the juices run clear when the thickest part of the meat is pierced with a skewer. If any bloody juices appear, cook for a little longer.

★ Let the chicken rest for 10 minutes before serving.

BARBECUED MEXICAN-STYLE GAME HENS ★

FOR THIS RECIPE, YOU'RE GOING TO SPATCHCOCK YOUR GAME HENS (POUSSINS). YOU MAY BE RELIEVED TO KNOW THAT THIS ISN'T SOME KIND OF HIGHLY INAPPROPRIATE GENITAL-RELATED EUPHEMISM, BUT INSTEAD REFERS TO OPENING THE BIRD OUT FLAT SO THAT IT COOKS QUICKLY AND EVENLY. SO NOW YOU KNOW. HAPPILY, IT'S EASILY DONE, SO GET INVOLVED WITH THE BUTCHERY, PEOPLE. JUST BE CAREFUL NOT TO CUT ANY MUCH-NEEDED DIGITS OFF. THE MARINADE USES SEXY, SPICY MEXICAN FLAVORS AND IS PERFECT SERVED WITH CREAMY CORN SALSA ON THE SIDE.

4 Cornish game hens (poussins)

1 recipe Corn and Pepper Salsa (page 15), to serve

Mexican marinade

4 jalapeño chile peppers

8 garlic cloves, peeled

4 tablespoons freshly squeezed orange juice

2 tablespoons freshly squeezed lime juice

1 tablespoon ground cumin

1 tablespoon dried oregano or thyme

2 teaspoons sea salt

⅓ cup (75 ml) olive oil

1 tablespoon maple syrup or clear honey

serves 4

★ To butterfly the birds, turn them breast side down and, using poultry shears or sturdy scissors, cut down each side of the backbone and discard it. Turn the birds over and open them out flat, pressing down hard on the breastbone. Thread 2 pre-soaked wooden skewers diagonally through each bird, from the wings to the thigh bones.

★ To make the marinade, skewer the chiles and garlic together and cook on a preheated medium–high grill/barbecue or under a broiler (grill) for 10 minutes, turning frequently, until evenly browned. Scrape off and discard the skins from the chiles and chop the flesh coarsely. Put the flesh and seeds into a food processor, add the garlic and all the remaining marinade ingredients, and blend to a paste.

★ Pour the marinade over the birds and let marinate in the refrigerator overnight. Return them to room temperature for 1 hour before cooking.

★ When ready to cook, remove the birds from their marinade and grill over medium–high preheated coals for 12 minutes on each side, basting occasionally. Remove from the heat, let rest for 5 minutes, then serve with the Corn and Pepper Salsa.

CHARGRILLED QUAIL
with kumquats

I BLOODY LOVE QUAIL. THERE'S SOMETHING INCREDIBLY INDULGENT ABOUT EATING A WHOLE BIRD YOURSELF, EVEN IF IT IS A MINI ONE. THEY CAN BE A BIT MESSY TO EAT, SO FOR EASE OF MUNCHING, IN THIS RECIPE THEY'RE BONED FIRST (OO-ER!). FILTHY. IF YOU FIND THE INCLUSION OF KUMQUATS RIDICULOUSLY EXOTIC OR SLIGHTLY PRETENTIOUS, AND YOU'RE TERRIFIED THAT YOUR BUDDIES WILL SNIGGER AT YOU, USE TANGERINE SEGMENTS INSTEAD.

4 quails, cleaned and boned (you can ask your butcher to do this)

2–3 tablespoons olive oil

freshly squeezed juice of 1 orange

2-inch (5-cm) piece fresh ginger, peeled and grated

a pinch of saffron threads

8 oz. (225 g) kumquats, halved

2 tablespoons honey

1 teaspoon paprika

a bunch of fresh cilantro (coriander), roughly chopped

serves 6

★ Thread 1 skewer through the wings of each quail and a second skewer through the thighs, so that each quail has 2 skewers through it. Put the quails in a shallow dish.

★ Mix the olive oil, orange juice, ginger, and saffron together in a bowl and smear the mixture over the quails. Cover with plastic wrap (clingfilm) and place in the refrigerator for 2–3 hours, turning the quails in the marinade from time to time.

★ Meanwhile, prepare the grill/barbecue and thread the kumquats onto the remaining skewers. Place the quails on the grill, brushing them with any leftover marinade, and cook them for about 4 minutes on each side. Halfway through the cooking time, put the kumquats on the grill with the quails and cook them until slightly charred.

★ Remove the quails and kumquats from the grill and serve immediately, drizzled with honey and sprinkled with the paprika and chopped cilantro (coriander).

SALMON
stuffed with herbs

AS I MAY ALREADY HAVE MENTIONED, COOKING A WHOLE FISH ON THE BARBECUE IS TRULY LOVELY, BUT WHAT ABOUT THE HEAD AND THE EYES? PERSONALLY, I'M NOT BOTHERED. BUT IF YOU'RE ONE OF THOSE PEOPLE WHO FIND IT DISTURBING TO HAVE YOUR DINNER'S DEAD EYES SIGHTLESSLY STARING BACK AT YOU IN AN ACCUSING MANNER, THEN HOW ABOUT THIS IDEA? CUT ITS FRIGGING HEAD OFF! IN FACT, WHILE YOU'RE AT IT, CUT ITS TAIL OFF, TOO. GET IT FILLETED, REMOVING THE CENTRAL BONE, AND TIE THE TWO FILLETS BACK TOGETHER. ET VOILA: AESTHETICALLY PLEASING AND NO GUILT TRIPS! IF YOU CAN'T MANAGE THIS HACK JOB YOURSELF, YOUR FISHMONGER SHOULD BE HAPPY TO HELP.

4 lb. (2 kg) whole salmon, filleted

1 stick (125 g) butter, softened

1 cup chopped, fresh soft-leaf mixed herbs, such as basil, chives, mint, parsley, and tarragon

grated zest of 1 unwaxed lemon

1 garlic clove, crushed

sea salt and freshly ground black pepper

olive oil, for brushing

kitchen twine

serves 8

★ Put the salmon fillets flat onto a board, flesh side up. Carefully pull out any remaining bones with tweezers.

★ Put the butter, herbs, lemon zest, garlic, and plenty of pepper into a small bowl and beat well. Spread the mixture over one of the salmon fillets and put the second on the top, arranging them top to tail.

★ Using kitchen twine, tie the fish together at 1-inch (2.5-cm) intervals. Brush with a little oil, sprinkle with salt and freshly ground black pepper, and cook on the flat plate of a grill/barbecue for 10 minutes on each side. Leave to rest for a further 10 minutes. Remove the twine and serve the fish cut into portions.

MOROCCAN BUTTERFLIED AND BARBECUED LAMB

IF YOU REALLY WANT TO COOK SOMETHING IMPRESSIVE ON THE BARBECUE, YOU CAN'T DO MUCH BETTER THAN THIS. A WHOLE LEG OF LAMB, BUTTERFLIED (CUT OPEN, BONES REMOVED, SO THAT IT'S BASICALLY FLAT AND OF EVEN THICKNESS—YOUR BUTCHER CAN DO THIS FOR YOU) AND RUBBED ALL OVER WITH BEAUTIFUL MOROCCAN FLAVORS, COOKED IN ONE PIECE ON THE BARBECUE. CUT IT INTO THIN SLICES AND FEED YOUR NO DOUBT CLAMORING GUESTS BY HAND, SEDUCTIVELY DANGLING EACH PIECE IN FRONT OF THEM BEFORE POPPING IT INTO THEIR WILLING MOUTHS. ERRR ... JUST ME THEN?

★ Trim any excess fat from the lamb and score the meat where necessary to make it the same thickness. Make deep slits all over the meat.

★ Put the peppercorns, coriander and cumin seeds, and paprika in a dry skillet or frying pan, toast for a couple minutes until aromatic, then grind or crush them. Transfer to a bowl, add the thyme, lime juice, garlic, yogurt, and salt to taste, then rub all over the cut side of the meat. Put in a shallow dish, cover, and let marinate in the refrigerator for at least 1 hour.

★ Grill the lamb skin side down over medium–high coals for 10–12 minutes, then turn and cook for a further 10–12 minutes for medium rare. (For medium, cook for a total of 30–35 minutes; for well done, cook for a total of 40 minutes.)

★ When cooked, remove from the heat, cover loosely with foil, and set aside in a warm place to rest for 10 minutes. Carve into long, thin slices. Serve with hot flatbreads, salad, and minted yogurt.

4-lb. (2-kg) leg of lamb, butterflied
1 tablespoon black peppercorns
1 tablespoon coriander seeds
1 tablespoon cumin seeds
1 tablespoon sweet Spanish paprika
2 teaspoons dried thyme
freshly squeezed juice of 1 lime
2 garlic cloves, crushed
½ cup (100 ml) plain yogurt
sea salt

to serve
broiled (grilled) flatbreads
salad
plain yogurt mixed with chopped fresh mint

serves 6–8

harissa and pomegranate
RACK OF LAMB

RACK OF LAMB IS A SUPERB CHOICE TO THROW ON THE BARBECUE, BECAUSE IT SOMEHOW MANAGES TO BE ALL THINGS TO ALL PEOPLE. IT CAN FEEL SUITABLY POSH AND DAINTY, IF THAT'S WHAT'S REQUIRED, YET AT THE SAME TIME IT'S BASICALLY MEAT ON A BONE—PRIMAL! HERE WE'RE GRILLING THE LAMB WITH THE NORTH AFRICAN FLAVORS OF HARISSA PASTE, FOR A CHILI KICK, AND POMEGRANATE, TO PROVIDE A BIT OF BALANCED SWEET AND SOUR.

2 whole racks of lamb

4 tablespoons Harissa (page 57)

1 tablespoon pomegranate molasses

seeds from 1 fresh pomegranate

serves 6

★ Rinse the lamb in cold water and pat dry with paper towels (kitchen paper). Cut the racks into double chops and place in a ceramic baking dish.

★ In a small bowl, mix together the harissa and pomegranate molasses and pour over the lamb. Rub into the meat, making sure it is well coated. Cover and refrigerate for 8–24 hours.

★ Remove the lamb from the fridge and stir to make sure all the sauce is on the meat. Allow the meat to come to room temperature.

★ Prepare a medium–high grill/barbecue. Put the lamb, skin side down, on the grill and cook for 5 minutes, then flip over. Reduce the heat to medium and cook for another 6–8 minutes. Cook for longer if you prefer your lamb well done.

★ Serve the chops sprinkled with the fresh pomegranate seeds.

TEX-MEX PORK RACK

DOES IT GET ANY BETTER THAN STUFFING YOUR FACE WITH A WHOLE RACK OF PORK SPARERIBS? SINGLE-MINDEDLY RIPPING OFF EACH INDIVIDUAL BONE, GREEDILY TEARING THE MEAT AWAY REGARDLESS THAT YOUR HANDS, FACE, CLOTHING, AND GENERAL SURROUNDING AREA ARE BEING SMOTHERED WITH SAUCE AS ONLOOKERS STARE AGHAST AT THE COMPLETE AND UTTER MEAT FIEND YOU SO OBVIOUSLY ARE. PERFECTION. HERE'S A NICE TEX-MEX-FLAVORED RECIPE: A BIT OF SPICE, A BIT OF SWEET, AND A BIT OF SOUR. NOTHING IS SET IN STONE, SO FEEL FREE TO ADAPT THE SPICE QUANTITIES TO SUIT YOUR OWN TASTE.

2 racks barbecue pork spareribs,
1 lb. (500 g) each

marinade

2 garlic cloves, crushed

2 tablespoons sea salt

2 tablespoons ground cumin

2 teaspoons chili powder

1 teaspoon dried oregano

8 tablespoons maple syrup or honey

4 tablespoons red wine vinegar

4 tablespoons olive oil

cornbread (or focaccia), to serve

serves 4–6

★ Wash the ribs and pat them dry with paper towels (kitchen paper). Transfer to a shallow, non-metal dish.

★ Put all the marinade ingredients into a bowl, mix well, pour over the ribs, then work in well with your hands. Cover and let marinate overnight in the refrigerator.

★ The next day, return the ribs to room temperature for 1 hour, then cook on a medium–high grill/barbecue for about 30 minutes, turning and basting frequently with the marinade juices. Cool a little, then serve with cornbread or focaccia.

Ingredients

8 chicken drumsticks and thighs, mixed, or 1 whole chicken, about 3 lb. (1.5 kg), cut into pieces

2 teaspoons sea salt

4 teaspoons smoked paprika or paprika

4 tablespoons extra virgin olive oil

3–4 boneless pork chops, or 12 oz. (350 g) salt pork cut into 1¼-inch (3-cm) cubes

2 onions, chopped

4 garlic cloves, crushed

1 lb. (500 g) tomatoes, fresh or canned, peeled, seeded, and chopped

2 large pinches of saffron threads, or 3 envelopes (sachets) ground saffron

1¾ cups (350 g) calasparra (paella) rice

3–3½ cups (750–800 ml) boiling chicken stock or water

1 cup (100 g) shelled fresh peas, or frozen peas, thawed

7 oz. (200 g) green beans, cut in half

8 baby artichokes, cut in half lengthwise, or canned or marinated equivalent

8 large uncooked shrimp (prawns), shell on

freshly ground black pepper

serves 4–6

PAELLA

THE VERY IDEA OF COOKING A PAELLA OUTDOORS, ON A BARBECUE, THAT WAFTING STEAM CLOUD OF SEAFOOD, RICE, AND CHICKEN AS IT BUBBLES AWAY IN A PAPRIKA-AND-SAFFRON-SPIKED BROTH OVER HOT COALS … WELL, I DON'T MIND SAYING THAT IT DOES THINGS TO ME, FRIENDS. EXCITING THINGS OF A SLIGHTLY ODD NATURE. I WON'T GO INTO IT HERE, BUT DON'T INVITE ME IF YOU'RE COOKING THIS—I MIGHT HAVE SOMEONE'S EYE OUT. MOVING ON … A QUICK, ER, TIP. DON'T STIR IT CONSTANTLY AS YOU WOULD A RISOTTO. NO.

★ Pat the chicken dry with paper towels (kitchen paper). Put the salt, pepper, and paprika in a bowl and mix well. Sprinkle the chicken with half the mixture and toss well.

★ Preheat a grill/barbecue to medium–high. Heat the oil in a large paella pan (a shallow skillet or frying pan will also do the job). Add the chicken and pork, in batches if necessary, and sauté over medium heat for 10–12 minutes, or until well browned. Remove with a slotted spoon and set aside.

★ Add the onions, garlic, tomatoes, and saffron to the pan, then add the remaining paprika mixture. Cook until thickened, about 5 minutes. Stir well, then return the meats to the pan and stir in the rice and most of the hot stock. Cook over high heat until bubbling fiercely, then reduce the heat and simmer gently, uncovered, for 15 minutes.

★ Add the peas, beans, artichokes, shrimp (prawns), and remaining stock, if necessary, and continue to cook for 10–15 minutes, or until the rice is cooked and glossy but dry. Serve the paella straight from the pan.

THAI LEMONGRASS QUAIL

QUAIL IS SO FRIGGING NICE! YEAH, IT'S A BIT DAINTY AND DELICATE, BUT AT THE SAME TIME IT'S PERFECT FOR RIPPING BITS OFF AND GREEDILY PICKING EVERY LAST SCRAP OF MEAT FROM THE BONES, GETTING YOUR FACE RIGHT IN THERE. WITH THIS RECIPE WE'RE USING THAI FLAVORS, ESPECIALLY LEMONGRASS—ITS SWEET, CITRUSSY NOTE WORKS VERY WELL WITH QUAIL. THESE WOULD BE PERFECT SERVED WITH A BOWL OF JASMINE RICE AND LIME WEDGES FOR SQUEEZING OVER. LOVELY.

8 quail, halved lengthwise along the backbones

1 recipe Thai Lemongrass Paste (see opposite)

6 limes, quartered, to serve

serves 4

★ Rinse the quail in cold water and pat dry with paper towels (kitchen paper). Put the birds in a ceramic baking dish and pour over the Thai Lemongrass Paste. Rub the paste into the quail on both sides, then cover and refrigerate for 6–8 hours, or overnight.

★ Remove the quail from the fridge and leave to come up to room temperature.

★ Prepare a medium–high grill/barbecue. Lay the quail on the grill, skin side down, and cook for 8 minutes per side, until cooked through. When done, remove from the grill, cover, and let stand for 10 minutes.

★ Serve the quail with lime wedges for squeezing over.

a 2-inch (5-cm) piece galangal, peeled and roughly chopped

2 lemongrass stalks, crushed and roughly chopped

6 Kaffir lime leaves

4 bird's eye chile peppers, roughly chopped

2 tablespoons honey

2 tablespoons Thai fish sauce

1 teaspoon Sriracha sauce or hot sauce

freshly squeezed juice and grated zest of 2 unwaxed limes

3 tablespoons vegetable oil

a large bunch of fresh cilantro (coriander), chopped

makes 1 cup (250 ml)

THAI LEMONGRASS PASTE

* Put all the ingredients in a blender or food processor and process to a thick paste.

* Store the paste in an airtight container in the fridge for up to 1 week.

* Use to season curries or rub on poultry before cooking. This paste can also be used on beef, pork, or fish.

CHAPTER 6

VEGGIE LEGENDS

MUSHROOM BURGERS with caramelized garlic aïoli

DESPITE BEING AN ABSOLUTELY RAMPANT MEAT-EATER—I MEAN, SERIOUSLY, I'M RARELY HAPPY UNLESS I'VE GOT A SEVERED MEDIUM-RARE HOOF HANGING OUT OF MY GOB (IDEALY SMOTHERED IN BÉARNAISE)—THE JUICY MEATINESS OF PORTOBELLO MUSHROOMS DONE ON THE BARBECUE AND SMOTHERED IN A RASPING GARLIC SAUCE CAN MAKE ME FORGET ALL ABOUT ANIMAL PARTS. ALMOST. IF YOU DON'T FANCY THE AÏOLI (WHAT D'YA MEAN YOU'RE NOT A FAN OF GARLIC?!), THESE ARE ALSO SUPERB WITH THE MORE TRADITIONAL BURGER ACCOMPANIMENTS OF MUSTARD, SALAD, CHEESE, AND PICKLES.

★ To make the aïoli, wrap the garlic head in foil and bake in a preheated oven at 400°F (200°C) for 45–50 minutes, until the garlic is really soft. Let cool, then squeeze the garlic purée out of each clove into a bowl.

★ Put the egg yolks, mustard, lemon juice, salt, and garlic purée in a food processor and blend briefly until frothy. With the motor running, gradually pour in the oil through the funnel until the sauce is thickened and all the oil incorporated. Transfer the aïoli to a bowl, cover the surface with plastic wrap (clingfilm), and chill until required.

★ Peel the mushroom caps and trim the stalks so they are flat with the cups. Brush lightly with olive oil, season with salt and pepper, and grill/barbecue for 4–5 minutes on each side until softened and cooked through.

★ Toast the buns and fill with the mushrooms, caramelized garlic aïoli, relish, and some arugula (rocket) leaves. Serve hot.

8 large portobello mushrooms

4–6 tablespoons olive oil

4 large burger buns, halved

4 tablespoons Chile Relish (page 53)

a handful of arugula (rocket) leaves

sea salt and freshly ground black pepper

caramelized garlic aïoli

1 large head garlic

2 egg yolks

1 teaspoon Dijon mustard

1 teaspoon freshly squeezed lemon juice

1 cup (200 ml) olive oil

serves 4

SESAME SWEET POTATO PACKETS

SWEET POTATOES ARE SUPERB BECAUSE THEY COOK QUICKLY WITHOUT NEEDING PRE-BOILING. JUST TOSS IN THE DRESSING, WRAP IN FOIL, AND THEY BASICALLY STEAM AND ABSORB THE FLAVORS. EASY-PEASY. THE ONLY THING YOU NEED TO WATCH OUT FOR IS THAT YOUR SWEET SPUDS DON'T BURN THROUGH THE FOIL, SO TRY TO AVOID DIRECT CONTACT WITH THE HEAT. THIS RECIPE SUGGESTS MAKING FOUR INDIVIDUAL PACKETS, BUT IF YOU CAN'T BE ARSED WITH ALL THAT, DO ONE LARGE PACKET; IT'LL COOK JUST AS WELL. THESE ARE PERFECT ACCOMPANIMENTS FOR ANY MEAT YOU MAY BE SERVING, SO DO THEM FIRST AND KEEP THEM WARM TO ONE SIDE OF THE BARBECUE.

4 large sweet potatoes, about 1¼ lb. (625 g), peeled and cut into 4 or 5 slices

1–2 tablespoons vegetable oil

1–2 tablespoons shoyu or tamari soy sauce

1 tablespoon sesame seeds

1 tablespoon finely chopped fresh flat leaf parsley, to serve

a grill/barbecue with a lid

serves 4

* Put the sweet potato in a bowl with the oil, soy sauce, and sesame seeds and toss well. Divide between 4 large squares of foil, then crinkle the foil up around them and close tightly. Put the foil packets on a preheated hot grill/barbecue, close the lid, and let cook for 20–30 minutes or until tender. Alternatively, place the foil packets on a baking sheet and bake in a preheated oven at 350°F (180°C) for 20 minutes or until tender.

* When ready to serve, open up the packets and sprinkle a little parsley on the sweet potatoes.

GRILLED EGGPLANT

with lemon, mint, and balsamic vinegar

EGGPLANT (AUBERGINE) HAS TO BE ONE OF MY FAVORITE VEGETABLES. IGNORING THE FACT THAT IT'S ABSOLUTELY DELICIOUS, ITS SHINY, PURPLE, BULBOUS PROFILE IS SOMEHOW INCREDIBLY COMFORTING AND PLEASING TO THE EYE. I REALLY HAVE NO IDEA WHY. HONEST! MOVING ON QUICKLY … THIS RECIPE REALLY IS RIDICULOUSLY EASY TO KNOCK OUT. IT'S IMPORTANT THAT YOU BASTE THE EGGPLANT SLICES WITH PLENTY OF OIL AND DON'T LET THEM GET TOO HOT, OTHERWISE THEY'LL BURN BEFORE THEY BROWN. WE'RE AIMING FOR A GENTLE SIZZLE. IF YOU FEEL THE MINT AND LEMON FLAVORS ARE A LITTLE TOO DELICATE, ADD SOME CRUSHED GARLIC. IF THAT'S NOT ENOUGH FOR YOU, I RECKON IT COULDN'T HURT TO CRUMBLE SOME FETA CHEESE OVER THE WHOLE LOT.

2 medium eggplant
(aubergines), about 14 oz.
(400 g)

regular olive oil, for basting

dressing

½ cup (100 ml) extra virgin
olive oil

finely grated zest and juice
of 1 ripe unwaxed lemon

2 tablespoons balsamic vinegar

1–2 teaspoons sugar

4 tablespoons very coarsely
chopped fresh mint leaves

sea salt and freshly ground
black pepper

serves 4

★ To make the dressing, put the oil, lemon juice and zest, and balsamic vinegar in a bowl and beat well. Add the sugar, salt, and pepper to taste—it should be fairly sweet. Stir in half the mint, then set aside until required.

★ Prepare the grill/barbecue. Cut each eggplant (aubergine) into 8 thin slices, brush lightly with olive oil, and cook for 2–3 minutes on each side, until golden brown and lightly charred. Arrange the slices on a large platter and spoon the dressing over the top. Cover and set aside so that the eggplant absorbs the flavors of the dressing. Sprinkle with the remaining chopped mint and serve.

SPICED FALAFEL BURGER

ORIGINATING IN EGYPT, FALAFELS CONSIST OF CHICKPEAS AND HERBS ROLLED INTO BITE-SIZE BALLS (OOOH) AND FRIED. NORMALLY STUFFED INTO WARM PITA BREAD WITH SALAD AND HUMMUS, THEY MAKE PRETTY DAMN FINE EATING. BUT WHATEVER … PITA-SHMITTA! LET'S STUFF THOSE BAD BOYS IN A FRIGGING BURGER BUN, AND INSTEAD OF HUMMUS LET'S SMOTHER THEM IN A TAHINI YOGURT SAUCE. HELL YEAH! FOR THIS RECIPE, THE FALAFEL NEED TO BE FRIED TO PREVENT THEM DRYING OUT, BUT THEY CAN BE FINISHED FOR A MINUTE OR TWO ON THE BARBECUE TO ADD SOME SEXY SMOKY FLAVORS. ONLY DO THIS IF YOU'VE ALREADY DRAGGED THE BARBECUE OUT FOR SOMETHING ELSE, THOUGH—OTHERWISE I'D SAY DON'T WORRY ABOUT IT.

1¼ cups (225 g) dried chickpeas

1 small onion, finely chopped

2 garlic cloves, crushed

½ bunch of fresh flat leaf parsley

½ bunch of fresh cilantro (coriander)

2 teaspoons ground coriander

½ teaspoon baking powder

4 hero (oval) rolls

a handful of salad leaves

2 tomatoes, diced

sea salt and freshly ground black pepper

peanut (groundnut), safflower, or sunflower oil, for shallow frying

tahini yogurt sauce

½ cup (100 ml) thick plain (Greek) yogurt

1 tablespoon tahini paste

1 garlic clove, crushed

½ tablespoon freshly squeezed lemon juice

1 tablespoon extra virgin olive oil

serves 4

★ Put the dried chickpeas in a bowl and add cold water to cover by at least 5 inches (12 cm). Let soak overnight. Drain the chickpeas well, transfer to a food processor, and blend until coarsely ground. Add the onion, garlic, parsley, cilantro (coriander), ground coriander, baking powder, and some salt and pepper and blend until very smooth. Transfer to a bowl, cover, and chill for 30 minutes.

★ To make the tahini sauce, put the yogurt, tahini, garlic, lemon juice, and olive oil in a bowl and whisk until smooth. Season to taste with salt and pepper and set aside until required.

★ Using wet hands, shape the chickpea mixture into 12 small or 8 medium patties. Heat a shallow layer of oil in a skillet or frying pan, add the patties, and fry for 3 minutes on each side until golden and cooked through. Drain on paper towels, then finish off on the grill for a couple of minutes max on each side.

★ Cut the rolls in half and fill with 2 or 3 patties, tahini yogurt sauce, salad leaves, and diced tomato. Serve hot.

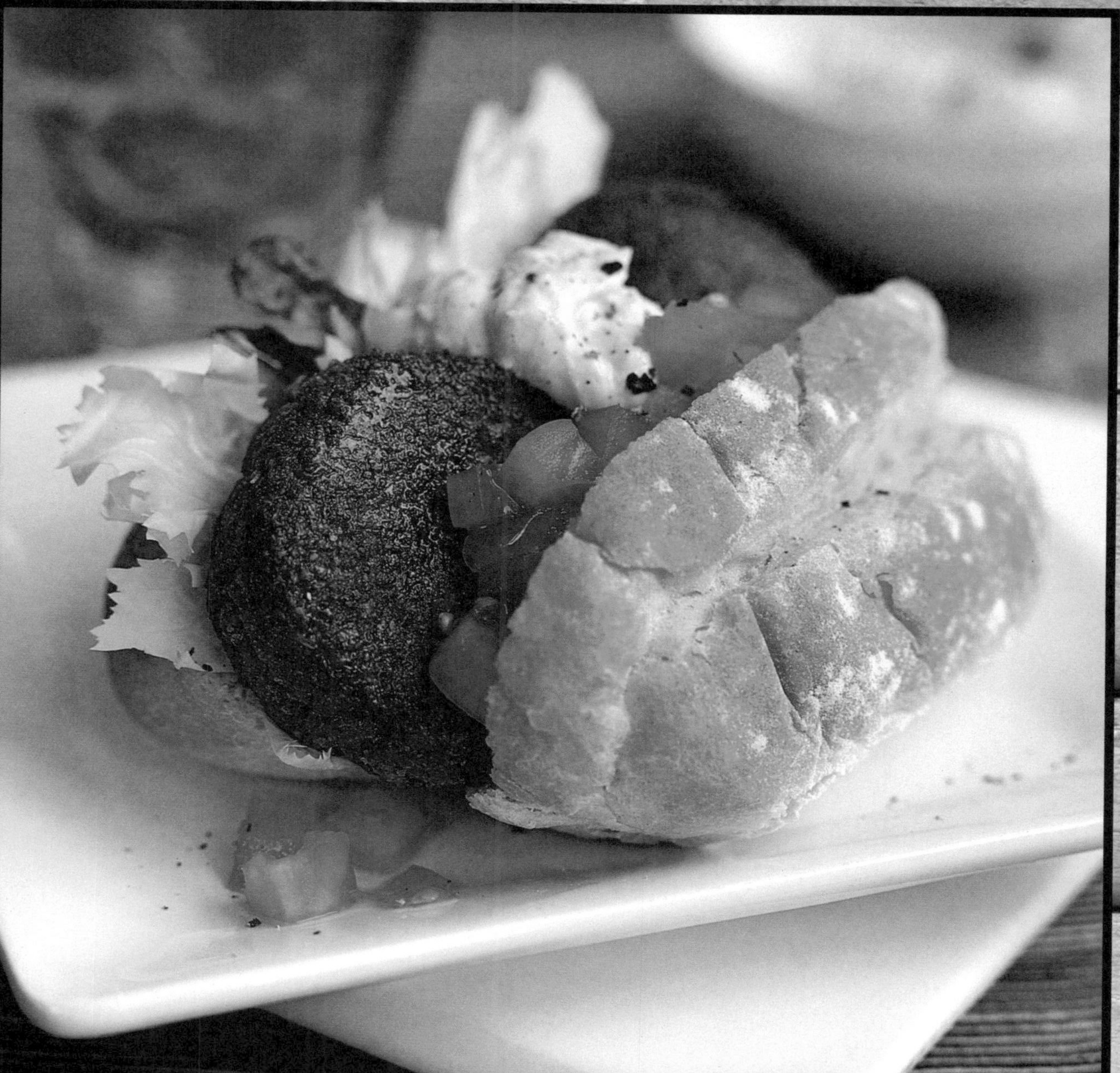

CHUNKY EGGPLANT BURGERS
with pesto

A BURGER WITH NO MEAT IN IT?, YOU ASK AGHAST—QUELLE HORREUR! BUT DON'T BE DUBIOUS. YEAH, I KNOW IT'S VEGETARIAN, BUT IT'S LOVELY. SERIOUSLY, HAVE I STEERED YOU WRONG SO FAR? NOPE, WELL, PROBABLY NOT THAT MUCH, BUT LET'S FORGET THAT ONE TIME (IT IS JUST ONE TIME, RIGHT?) SWEEP IT ALL UNDER THE CARPET AND START AGAIN IN A NEUTRAL POSITION OF LOVE AND TRUST. BELIEVE IT. SO NOW WE'VE GOT THAT OUT OF THE WAY, LET'S TALK ABOUT THE ACTUAL RECIPE. HERE, THE MEAT IN THE BURGER IS REPLACED WITH SMOKY EGGPLANT (AUBERGINE), WHICH, WHEN COMBINED WITH THE FRESH BASIL TASTE OF THE PESTO, CREATES A SUPER MEDITERRANEAN VIBE.

1 large eggplant (aubergine), about 1½ lb. (750 g)

4 tablespoons extra virgin olive oil

1 tablespoon balsamic vinegar

1 garlic clove, crushed

4 soft bread rolls, halved

2 beefsteak tomatoes, thickly sliced

7 oz. (200 g) mozzarella, sliced

a handful of arugula (rocket) leaves

sea salt and freshly ground black pepper

pesto

1½ cups (50 g) fresh basil leaves

1 garlic clove, crushed

4 tablespoons pine nuts

7 tablespoons extra virgin olive oil

2 tablespoons freshly grated Parmesan cheese

serves 4

★ To make the pesto, put the basil, garlic, pine nuts, oil, and some salt and pepper in a food processor and blend until fairly smooth. Transfer to a bowl, stir in the Parmesan, and add more salt and pepper to taste. Set aside until required.

★ Cut the eggplant (aubergine) into ½-inch (1-cm) slices. Put the oil, vinegar, garlic, salt, and pepper in a bowl, whisk to mix, then brush over the eggplant slices. Cook them on a preheated hot grill/barbecue for 3–4 minutes on each side until charred and softened.

★ Lightly toast the rolls and top with a slice of eggplant. Spread with pesto, add another slice of eggplant, then add a slice each of tomato and mozzarella. Drizzle with more pesto, then top with a few arugula (rocket) leaves. Put the tops on the rolls and serve hot.

PLANTAIN
with lime and chili

2 plantains, thinly sliced diagonally

freshly squeezed juice of 1 lime

1 tablespoon chili oil

sea salt

fresh cilantro (coriander), coarsely
chopped, to serve

serves 4

IF YOU LOOK AT A PLANTAIN IT'S VERY OBVIOUSLY A TYPE OF BANANA. THE DIFFERENCE IS THAT IT'S STARCHY, NOT AT ALL SWEET COMPARED TO YOUR EVERYDAY BANANA, AND PRETTY MUCH INEDIBLE UNLESS IT'S COOKED. PLANTAIN WORKS PARTICULARLY WELL ON BARBECUES OR GRILLS: THE CHARGRILLING BRINGS OUT WHAT SWEETNESS THERE IS AND THAT'S COMPLEMENTED NICELY WITH A BIT OF CITRUS AND A CHILI KICK. SERIOUSLY, GIVE THIS RECIPE A GO—IT'S THE BEST KIND AS THERE'S SOD-ALL WORK INVOLVED AND IT TAKES MINUTES TO COOK.

★ Put the slices of plantain in a large bowl with the lime juice and chile oil. Carefully turn them over to cover evenly (this will stop them discoloring).

★ Arrange the slices on a preheated grill/barbecue and cook for 2–3 minutes or until slightly charred. Gently turn them over, using a palette knife, then cook the other side for 2 minutes. (The plantain changes from a fleshy color to a beautiful bright yellow blackened with the stripes of the grill.)

★ When cooked, lift onto a plate, sprinkle with salt and cilantro (coriander), then serve.

1½ lb. (750 g) baby leeks, trimmed

2–3 tablespoons extra virgin olive oil

sea salt

a few lemon wedges, to serve

tarator sauce

2 oz. (50 g) macadamia nuts, toasted

scant ½ cup (25 g) fresh bread crumbs

2 garlic cloves, crushed

½ cup (100 ml) extra virgin olive oil

1 tablespoon freshly squeezed lemon juice

sea salt and freshly ground black pepper

serves 4

CHARRED LEEKS
with tarator sauce

VEGETABLES OF ALL TYPES, SHAPES, AND SIZES ARE ABSOLUTELY GORGEOUS CHARGRILLED ON THE BARBECUE. THE SMOKY BURNT FLAVOR THIS METHOD OF COOKING IMPARTS IS AMAZING. LEEKS ARE PARTICULARLY GOOD DONE THIS WAY, AND IF YOU DRIZZLE THEM WITH THE MIDDLE EASTERN NUT SAUCE TARATOR YOU HAVE AN UNBEATABLE COMBINATION. REPLACING THE BABY LEEKS WITH SCALLIONS (SPRING ONIONS) WOULD WORK JUST AS WELL. SIMPLE AND DELICIOUS.

★ To make the sauce, put the nuts in a food processor and grind coarsely, then add the bread crumbs, garlic, and salt and pepper, and process again to form a smooth paste. Transfer to a bowl and very gradually beat in the olive oil, lemon juice, and 2 tablespoons boiling water to form a sauce. Season to taste with salt and pepper.

★ Preheat the grill/barbecue. Brush the leeks with a little olive oil, season with salt, and cook over medium–high coals for 6–10 minutes, turning occasionally, until charred and tender. Transfer to a plate, sprinkle with olive oil, then pour the sauce over the top. Serve with lemon wedges.

SPICY TOFU SATAY

with soy dipping sauce

NOW, THERE'S A CHANCE YOU MIGHT READ THE TITLE OF THIS RECIPE AND THINK "WHAT THE HELL? I AIN'T EATING NO DAMN TOFU, THAT'S FOR VEGGIES AND VARIOUS OTHER MISGUIDED DEVOTEES OF THE MUNG BEAN!" AND YOU KNOW WHAT, THAT WOULD HAVE BEEN ME A FEW YEARS BACK. BUT A FRIEND OF MINE, ELLY, WHO'S AN EXCELLENT COOK (AND VEGETARIAN, BUT WE WON'T HOLD THAT AGAINST HER), TAUGHT ME OTHERWISE. TOFU IS PROBABLY MORE ABOUT ITS UNUSUAL TEXTURE THAN TASTE, AND BECAUSE IT'S OFTEN FAIRLY BLAND (ALTHOUGH SMOKED TOFU IS BANGING STRAIGHT OUT OF THE PACK), IT TAKES ON OTHER FLAVORS REALLY WELL—IN THIS CASE, VIETNAMESE. TRY IT, IT'S BLOODY NICE.

★ To make the marinade, mix the lemongrass, groundnut (peanut) oil, soy sauce, chile, garlic, and turmeric with the sugar until it has dissolved. Add a little salt to taste and toss in the tofu, making sure it is well coated. Leave to marinate for 1 hour.

★ Prepare the soy dipping sauce by whisking all the ingredients together. Set aside until ready to serve.

★ Preheat the grill/barbecue. Thread the tofu cubes onto pre-soaked wooden skewers and grill them for 2–3 minutes on each side. Serve the tofu hot, garnished with the shredded basil and with the dipping sauce on the side.

10 oz. (280 g) firm tofu, rinsed, drained, patted dry, and cut into bite-size cubes

leaves from a small bunch of fresh basil, shredded

sesame oil, for frying

marinade

3 lemongrass stalks, trimmed and finely chopped

1 tablespoon groundnut (peanut) oil

3 tablespoons soy sauce

1–2 fresh red chile peppers, seeded and finely chopped

2 garlic cloves, crushed

1 teaspoon ground turmeric

2 teaspoons sugar

sea salt

soy dipping sauce

4–5 tablespoons soy sauce

1–2 tablespoons Thai fish sauce

freshly squeezed juice of 1 lime

1–2 teaspoons sugar

1 fresh red chile pepper, seeded and finely chopped

serves 3–4

GRILLED CORN ON THE COB

CORN ON THE COB IS ABSOLUTELY BANGING ON THE BARBECUE. ALL YOU REALLY NEED IS TO THROW THE HUSKS ON AND CHAR THEM ALL OVER. IT'S NO EFFORT AT ALL, ALTHOUGH THIS RECIPE (IF YOU CAN REALLY CALL IT THAT) FINISHES THE COOKED COBS OFF IN MEXICAN FASHION, RUBBED WITH LIME AND SPRINKLED WITH CHILI OR PAPRIKA. IF EVEN THAT SEEMS LIKE TOO MUCH EFFORT, THEY'RE PRETTY DAMN GOOD JUST SLATHERED WITH BUTTER. IF YOU GO DOWN THIS ROUTE, DON'T SMOTHER THEM IN HERB BUTTER FROM THE FRIDGE LEFTOVER FROM A DIFFERENT RECIPE, FORGETTING IT HAS ANCHOVIES IN IT. ANCHOVY AND CORN IS A FLAVOR COMBINATION TO BE AVOIDED AT ALL COSTS, PEOPLE.

4 whole corn cobs, husks and stray strands removed, then thoroughly washed and dried

2 limes, quartered

sea salt

1 teaspoon medium chili powder/ground red chili or paprika

serves 4

* Preheat the grill/barbecue to high.

* Grill the cobs, turning regularly, for 15–20 minutes or until charred all over.

* Remove from the grill with tongs and rub lime wedges over each cob.

* Generously sprinkle each cob with salt and chili powder/ground chili or paprika to taste.

BEET AND PEARL ONION BROCHETTES

BROCHETTE IS A FANCY FRENCH TERM FOR COOKING STUFF ON SKEWERS. KIND OF GOOD TO KNOW IF YOU WANT TO IMPRESS PEOPLE WHO LIKE THAT SORT OF THING, BUT IF YOU'RE THROWING THESE ON THE BARBECUE FOR A ROWDY BUNCH OF VEGETARIAN BUDDIES (IF THERE IS SUCH A THING), THEN MAYBE CALL THEM KEBABS, SO THEY DON'T SNIGGER AT YOU BEHIND YOUR BACK FOR SUCH RIDICULOUS PRETENTIOUSNESS. THE PITFALLS OF WHAT TO CALL THIS DISH ASIDE, YOU NEED BEETS (BEETROOT) AND BABY ONIONS OF ROUGHLY THE SAME SIZE, SO THEY COOK EVENLY. IF YOU HAVE NO VEGGIE FRIENDS, THIS IS A GREAT ACCOMPANIMENT TO ALL SORTS OF MORE TRADITIONAL MEATY BARBECUE GRUB.

32 large fresh bay leaves

20 small beets (beetroot)

20 pearl (baby) onions, unpeeled

3 tablespoons extra virgin olive oil

1 tablespoon balsamic vinegar

sea salt and freshly ground black pepper

8 metal skewers

serves 4

★ Put the bay leaves into a bowl, cover with cold water, and let soak for 1 hour before cooking.

★ Cut the stalks off the beets (beetroot) and wash well under cold running water. Put the beets and pearl (baby) onions into a large pan of lightly salted boiling water and blanch for 5 minutes. Drain and refresh under cold running water. Pat dry with paper towels (kitchen paper), then peel the onions.

★ Preheat the barbecue/grill. Thread the beets, onions, and damp bay leaves onto the skewers, sprinkle with the olive oil and vinegar, and season well with salt and pepper. Cook over medium–hot coals for 20–25 minutes, turning occasionally, until charred and tender, then serve.

ROASTED BELL PEPPER AND ASPARAGUS

ASPARAGUS IS ABSOLUTELY BANGING! WHEN IT'S IN SEASON YOU SHOULD BE EATING AS MUCH OF IT AS YOU CAN STUFF IN YOUR FACE, EVEN IF IT'S SIMPLY CHARGRILLED, SEASONED WITH FLAKY SEA SALT AND PEPPER AND A SQUEEZE OF LEMON. DON'T BOTHER EATING ASPARAGUS THAT'S NOT LOCAL TO YOU—IT'LL BE CRAP AND BAD FOR THE ENVIRONMENT. HERE, WE'RE FIRING THE ASPARAGUS WITH SWEET RED BELL PEPPERS (RAMIRO OR ROMANO, PREFERABLY), AND TOSSING THE WHOLE LOT IN A HAZELNUT-OIL DRESSING. THIS SALAD SERVES FOUR AS A MAIN OR SIX AS AN APPETIZER. I RECKON IT WOULD BE EXTRA SUPERB WITH A POACHED EGG ON EACH PORTION.

½ red onion, sliced

6 red bell peppers

1 lb. (500 g) asparagus spears, trimmed

extra virgin olive oil, for brushing

8 oz. (225 g) snowpeas (mangetout)

4 oz. (125 g) mixed salad leaves

a handful of fresh parsley and dill leaves

2 oz. (50 g) hazelnuts, toasted and coarsely chopped

hazelnut oil dressing

4 tablespoons hazelnut oil

2 tablespoons extra virgin olive oil

1 tablespoon sherry vinegar

1 teaspoon sugar

sea salt and freshly ground black pepper

serves 4–6

★ Put the sliced onion into a strainer (sieve), sprinkle with salt, and let drain over a bowl for 30 minutes. Rinse in cold running water and pat dry with paper towels (kitchen paper).

★ Prepare the grill/barbecue, then cook the bell peppers over hot coals for 15 minutes, turning frequently, until charred all over. Transfer to a plastic bag, seal, and let soften until cool. Peel off the skin and discard the seeds, then cut the flesh into thick strips.

★ Brush the asparagus with olive oil and cook over hot coals for 3–4 minutes, turning frequently, until charred and tender.

★ Put the snowpeas (mangetout) in a large pan of lightly salted boiling water and boil for 1–2 minutes. Drain and refresh under cold running water.

★ Put the onion, peppers, asparagus, and snowpeas into a large bowl and toss gently. Add the salad leaves, herbs, and hazelnuts. Put the dressing ingredients into a bowl, whisk well, then pour over the salad and toss until coated. Serve.

GRILLED PITA SALAD
with olive salsa and mozzarella

8 oz. (225 g) fresh mozzarella cheese, drained

1 large green bell pepper, seeded and chopped

1 Lebanese (mini) cucumber, chopped

2 ripe tomatoes, chopped

½ red onion, finely chopped

2 pita breads

4 tablespoons extra virgin olive oil

freshly squeezed juice of ½ lemon

sea salt and freshly ground black pepper

olive salsa

3 oz. (75 g) Kalamata olives, pitted and chopped

1 tablespoon chopped fresh parsley

1 small garlic clove, finely chopped

4 tablespoons extra virgin olive oil

1 tablespoon freshly squeezed lemon juice

freshly ground black pepper

serves 4

WHO KNEW YOU COULD FLASH FRESH MOZZARELLA CHEESE ON THE BARBECUE? YEAH, WELL, IT TURNS OUT YOU CAN, AND IT TAKES ON A LOVELY SMOKINESS. BUT ONLY DO IT FOR ONE MINUTE PER SIDE TOPS, OR I RECKON YOU'LL BE WATCHING YOUR EXPENSIVE BALL OF CHEESE DRIBBLING THROUGH THE BARS OF THE GRILL. OF COURSE, YOU DON'T EVEN NEED TO COOK THE CHEESE, JUST RIP IT UP AND THROW IT IN. IF MOZZARELLA DOESN'T FLOAT YOUR BOAT, YOU COULD USE HALLOUMI INSTEAD, FOR A FIRMER VIBE. WHATEVER YOU USE, GIVE THE SLICES A RUB WITH SOME OLIVE OIL FIRST: PRYING OFF CHEESE THAT'S STUCK FAST TO THE GRILL IS NO FUN AT ALL.

★ Wrap the mozzarella in paper towels (kitchen paper) and squeeze gently to remove excess water. Unwrap and cut into thick slices. Brush the slices well with olive oil and place them on the grill/barbecue. Cook over hot coals for 1 minute on each side until the cheese is charred with lines and beginning to soften. Alternatively, simply slice the cheese and use without grilling.

★ Put the green bell pepper, cucumber, tomatoes, and onion into a bowl. Toast the pita breads over hot coals, cool slightly, then tear into bite-size pieces. Add to the bowl, then pour over the olive oil and lemon juice. Season and stir well.

★ Put all the ingredients for the olive salsa into a bowl and stir well.

★ Spoon the salad onto small plates, top with a few slices of mozzarella and some olive salsa, then serve.

EGGPLANT AND SMOKED CHEESE ROLLS

HERE WE HAVE A CLASSY, SOPHISTICATED CANAPÉ-TYPE BARBECUE DISH, ONE TO BRING OUT WHEN THE PARTNER'S PARENTS OR THE BOSS IS AROUND. IT'S BASICALLY CHARGRILLED EGGPLANT (AUBERGINE) SLICES STUFFED WITH HERBS AND SMOKED CHEESE, WHICH WILL MELT INSIDE THE HOT ROLLED VEGETABLE. SEXUAL. TO REINFORCE THAT CLASSY EDGE TO YOUR EVENT, DON'T FORGET TO THROW A COUPLE BOXES OF FERRERO ROCHER INTO THE MIX FOR DESSERT. I SUGGEST SERVING THEM ON A SILVER PLATTER, PILED INTO A PYRAMID.

2 eggplant (aubergines), cut lengthwise into about 5 slices

1 teaspoon chili oil

½ cup (100 ml) olive oil

3 teaspoons cumin seeds, lightly toasted in a dry skillet (frying pan) and ground

2 garlic cloves, crushed

1 fresh red chile pepper, seeded and finely chopped

a large handful of fresh mint leaves, finely chopped

8 oz. (225 g) firm smoked cheese, sliced

sea salt and freshly ground black pepper

a large handful of fresh cilantro (coriander), coarsely chopped, to serve

freshly squeezed juice of ½ lemon, to serve

makes 10 rolls

* Arrange the eggplant (aubergine) slices on a large tray. Mix the olive and chili oils, cumin, garlic, chile, mint, salt, and pepper in a measuring cup (jug), then pour over the eggplant. Turn each slice over so that both sides are well coated. Cover with plastic wrap (clingfilm) and set aside for a few hours or overnight to soak up the flavors.

* Put the eggplant on a preheated grill/barbecue. Cook for about 4 minutes, then turn and cook the other side until tender and browned.

* Remove from the heat, put some of the cheese at one end of a slice of eggplant, and roll up firmly (do this while the eggplant is still hot, so that the cheese melts). Repeat with the other slices. Sprinkle with the cilantro (coriander) and lemon juice, and serve.

VEGETABLE ANTIPASTO

IT'S ALL WELL AND GOOD BARBECUING AND SERVING HUGE LUMPS OF MEAT TO YOUR ASSEMBLED GUESTS. I KNOW "MAN MAKES FIRE" AND THAT HUNTER-GATHERER VIBE IS UNIVERSALLY APPEALING, OBVIOUSLY, BUT YOU DON'T WANT TO BE TOTALLY PIGEONHOLED AS CRO-MAGNON MAN (OR WOMAN). NO. YOU ALSO NEED TO SHOW YOUR SENSITIVE, SOPHISTICATED SIDE. THE BEST WAY TO DO THIS IS BY SERVING A LARGE PLATTER OF GRILLED VEGETABLES ON THE SIDE. IT TAKES NO TIME AT ALL. JUST CHOOSE YOUR FAVORITES (IF YOU HAVE ANY). IF YOU WANT TO BE EXTRA-SENSITIVE/SOPHISTICATED, PILE THEM ON A BED OF POLENTA. JOB DONE. NOW GO BACK TO EATING A GREAT BIG JUICY RIB.

★ Cut the bell peppers into quarters and remove and discard the seeds. Trim the fennel, reserving the fronds, and cut the bulbs into ¼-inch (5-mm) slices. Cut the eggplant (aubergine) into thick slices and cut in half again. Cut the zucchini (courgettes) into thick slices diagonally and cut the onion into wedges.

★ Put all the vegetables in a large bowl, add the marinade, and toss gently until evenly coated. Cover and let marinate in a cool place for at least 1 hour.

★ Preheat the grill/barbecue, then cook the vegetables on the grill rack until they are tender and lightly charred. Let cool, then peel the bell peppers.

★ Arrange the vegetables on a large platter, sprinkle with the herbs, the reserved fennel fronds, olive oil, and lemon juice, then season lightly with salt and pepper.

★ Serve at room temperature with crusty bread or grilled polenta.

2 red bell peppers

4 baby fennel bulbs

1 large eggplant (aubergine)

2 large zucchini (courgettes)

1 red onion

1 recipe Herb, Lemon, and Garlic Marinade (page 11)

a few fresh herb leaves, such as basil, dill, fennel, mint, and parsley

extra virgin olive oil, to taste

freshly squeezed lemon juice, to taste

sea salt and freshly ground black pepper

bread or grilled polenta, to serve

serves 4

SUMMER VEGETABLE KEBABS
with homemade garlicky pesto

2 eggplant (aubergines) and 2 zucchini (courgettes), cut into chunks

2–3 bell peppers, stalks removed, seeded, and cut into chunks

12–16 cherry tomatoes

4 red onions, cut into quarters

marinade

4 tablespoons olive oil

freshly squeezed juice of ½ lemon

2 garlic cloves, crushed

1 teaspoon sea salt

garlicky pesto

3–4 garlic cloves, roughly chopped

leaves from a large bunch of fresh basil (at least 30–40 leaves)

½ teaspoon sea salt

2–3 tablespoons pine nuts

extra virgin olive oil, as required

¼ cup (60 g) freshly grated Parmesan cheese

4–6 metal or wooden skewers, soaked in water before use

serves 4–6

YEAH, YEAH. VEGETABLES ON A STICK. I KNOW, YAWN. BUT THIS IS NICE BECAUSE THE VEG IS DRIZZLED WITH HOMEMADE PESTO. DON'T EVER BUY THE SUPERMARKET STUFF IN JARS, IT'S UNIVERSALLY AWFUL. ALWAYS MAKE YOUR OWN. IT'S LOVELY, AND IT CAN BE USED IN SO MANY WAYS—TOSSED THROUGH PASTA, SPLODGED ON GRILLED MEAT OR FISH—SO MAKE LOADS. IT KEEPS FOR A GOOD FEW DAYS IN THE FRIDGE AS LONG AS THE SURFACE IS COVERED WITH OIL. THIS VERSION USES A BIT MORE GARLIC THAN USUAL (HENCE THE NAME), BUT IT'S ENTIRELY UP TO YOU HOW MUCH YOU PUT IN. IF YOU PLAN ON KISSING SOMEONE, A HALF OR SINGLE CLOVE IS MORE LIKE THE USUAL AMOUNT.

★ To make the pesto, use a mortar and pestle to pound the garlic with the basil leaves and salt—the salt will act as an abrasive and help to grind. (If you only have a small mortar and pestle, you may have to do this in batches.) Add the pine nuts and pound them to a paste. Slowly drizzle in some olive oil and bind with the grated Parmesan. Continue to pound and grind with the pestle, adding in enough oil to make a smooth sauce. Set aside.

★ Put all the prepared vegetables in a bowl. Mix together the olive oil, lemon juice, garlic, and salt and pour it over the vegetables. Using your hands, toss the vegetables gently in the marinade, then thread them onto the skewers.

★ Preheat the grill/barbecue. Cook the kebabs for 2–3 minutes on each side, until the vegetables are nicely browned. Serve the kebabs with the pesto on the side for drizzling.

GRILLED ROSEMARY FLATBREAD

IMAGINE THE COMBINED SMELLS OF BAKING BREAD, BARBECUE SMOKE, AND ROSEMARY. HOLY MOLY, I DON'T KNOW ABOUT YOU, FRIENDS, BUT THE VERY IDEA OF INSERTING MY SNOUT INTO THE AIR AND GETTING A WAFT OF THAT LOT, WELL IT REALLY DOES SOMETHING FOR ME. NOW IMAGINE YOU'VE COOKED SOME STEAK OR SOME LAMB ON THE BARBECUE. IT'S SLICED UP INTO RAGGED RIBBONS AND NOW YOU'RE JUST LIFTING THE WARM BREAD—WHICH YOU'VE MADE YOURSELF—OFF THE GRILL TO PILE UP WITH A FISTFUL OF MEAT, SOAKING UP ALL THOSE MEATY JUICES *EYES ROLL BACK INTO HEAD* SERIOUSLY, WHY ARE YOU STILL EVEN READING THIS? GET THAT BARBECUE FIRED UP AND MAKE SOME FLATBREAD!

1¾ cups (250 g) white bread (strong) flour, plus extra for dusting

1½ teaspoons active (fast-acting) dry yeast

1 teaspoon salt

1 tablespoon chopped fresh rosemary

2 tablespoons extra virgin olive oil, plus extra for brushing

serves 4

★ Sift the flour into the bowl of an electric mixer and stir in the yeast, salt, and rosemary. Add ½ cup (120 ml) hot water and the olive oil and knead with the dough hook at high speed for about 8 minutes or until the dough is smooth and elastic.

★ Alternatively, sift the flour into a large bowl and stir in the yeast, salt, and rosemary. Make a well in the center, then add the hot water and olive oil and mix to form a soft dough. Turn out onto a lightly floured work surface and knead until the dough is smooth and elastic.

★ Shape the dough into a ball, then put into an oiled bowl, cover with a dish towel, and let rise in a warm place for 45–60 minutes or until doubled in size.

★ Punch down (knock back) the dough and divide into quarters. Roll out each piece on a lightly floured work surface to make a 6-inch-long (15-cm) oval.

★ Preheat the grill/barbecue to a low heat. Brush the bread with a little olive oil and cook for 5 minutes, then brush the top with the remaining olive oil, flip, and cook for a further 4–5 minutes until the bread is cooked through. Serve hot.

ZUCCHINI, FETA, AND MINT SALAD

1 tablespoon sesame seeds

6 large zucchini (courgettes)

3 tablespoons extra virgin olive oil

5 oz. (150 g) feta cheese, crumbled

a handful of fresh mint leaves

dressing

4 tablespoons extra virgin olive oil

1 tablespoon lemon juice

1 small garlic clove, crushed

sea salt and freshly ground black pepper

serves 4

THIS IS A NICE LITTLE SUMMER SALAD THAT YOU CAN EASILY KNOCK OUT IN NO TIME AT ALL. HAPPILY, IT WORKS WELL WITH BARBECUED MEAT OR FISH AND IS GOOD FOR ANY VEGETARIANS WHO MIGHT HAPPEN TO BE LURKING, TOO, SO YOU CAN'T LOSE. IT'S ACTUALLY SO QUICK TO MAKE—AS LONG AS YOU'VE DONE A BIT OF THE PREP—THAT YOU COULD START THROWING IT TOGETHER WHILE YOUR MEAT IS RESTING. SUPERB.

★ Put the sesame seeds into a dry skillet or frying pan and toast over medium heat until golden and aromatic. Remove from the heat, let cool, and set aside until required.

★ Preheat the grill/barbecue. Cut the zucchini (courgettes) diagonally into thick slices, toss with the olive oil, and season with salt and pepper. Cook over hot coals for 2–3 minutes on each side until charred and tender. Remove and let cool.

★ Put all the dressing ingredients into a screw-top jar and shake well. Add salt and pepper to taste.

★ Put the zucchini, feta, and mint into a large bowl, add the dressing, and toss well until evenly coated. Sprinkle with the sesame seeds and serve immediately.

EMBER-ROASTED POTATOES

I ABSOLUTELY LOVE A SIMPLE JACKET POTATO. ALTHOUGH I SAY "SIMPLE," IT STILL HAS TO BE COOKED JUST RIGHT. OBVIOUSLY. IT'S GOT TO HAVE CRISPY SKIN, THE INSIDES FORKED UP AND FLUFFY, SOAKING UP A SENSUOUSLY MELTING, DONKEY-CHOKING SLAB OF BUTTER AND A GOOD HANDFUL OF STRONG CHEDDAR CHEESE. HAPPILY, THE ABSOLUTE BEST JACKET POTATOES YOU CAN SCOFF ARE PROBABLY THE EASIEST TO DO. JUST WRAP 'EM IN FOIL AND LEAVE THEM IN THE EMBERS OF THE BARBECUE WHILE YOU'RE FIDDLING AROUND PRODDING YOUR MEAT ON THE GRILL ABOVE. AHEM. THAT'S IT, APART FROM TURNING THEM OVER HALFWAY THROUGH. IT'S ALMOST TOO EASY.

★ Prepare the grill/barbecue. Wrap the potatoes individually in a double layer of foil and, as soon as the coals are glowing red, put the potatoes on top. Rake the charcoal up and around them, but without covering them. Cook for about 25 minutes, then, using tongs, turn the potatoes over carefully and cook for a further 25–30 minutes until cooked through.

★ Remove from the heat and carefully remove the foil, then cut the potatoes in half. Serve, topped with a spoonful of butter, salt, and pepper.

4 medium baking potatoes

butter

sea salt and freshly ground black pepper

serves 4

GRILLED FIG AND PROSCIUTTO BRUSCHETTA
with arugula

4 thick slices of country bread,
preferably sourdough

2 garlic cloves, cut in half

extra virgin olive oil, for sprinkling
and brushing

8 ripe fresh figs

2 tablespoons balsamic vinegar

12 slices of prosciutto

1 cup (75 g) arugula (rocket)

sea salt and freshly ground
black pepper

shavings of Parmesan cheese,
to serve

serves 4

A PERFECTLY RIPE FIG IS JUST BEAUTIFUL, ONE OF THE NICEST THINGS YOU CAN EAT. I SAY THIS HAVING, IN THE PAST, TUCKED INTO UNDER-RIPE, PLASTIC-WRAPPED, TASTELESS FIGS THAT MANY SUPERMARKETS SEEM TO SPECIALIZE IN. IN FACT, I WAS ALMOST PUT OFF EATING FIGS ENTIRELY BY THESE POOR SPECIMENS, AS I JUST COULDN'T SEE WHAT THE FUSS WAS ABOUT. IT WASN'T TILL I ATE A PROPER, JAMMY, TASTY FIG ON VACATION ONE YEAR THAT EVERYTHING CHANGED. SO MAKE SURE YOUR FIGS ARE RIPE, OK? IT'S BEST TO GET THEM FROM A GREENGROCER, WHERE YOU CAN HANDLE THE GOODS. BY THE WAY, FOR THIS RECIPE WE'RE GOING TO BE CARAMELIZING THE FIGS ON THE BARBECUE AND SERVING THEM WITH CRISPY PROSCIUTTO. LOVELY.

★ To make the bruschetta, broil (grill), toast, or pan-grill the bread on both sides until lightly browned or toasted. Rub the top side of each slice with the cut garlic, then sprinkle with olive oil. Keep in a warm oven.

★ Stand the figs upright. Using a small, sharp knife, make two cuts across each fig, not quite quartering it, but keeping it intact at the base. Ease the figs open and brush with balsamic vinegar and olive oil. Put the figs, cut side down, on a preheated grill/barbecue and cook for 3–4 minutes until hot and slightly browned—don't move them during cooking.

★ While the figs are cooking, place half the slices of prosciutto on the barbecue and cook until frazzled. Remove and keep warm while cooking the remaining slices. Place two figs, three pieces of prosciutto, and some arugula (rocket) on each slice of bruschetta. Cover with Parmesan shavings and sprinkle with olive oil. Season to taste with salt and pepper and serve immediately.

GRILLED POLENTA

POLENTA IS A RATHER LOVELY THING. THIS ITALIAN CORNMEAL CAN BE MIXED UP AND SERVED IN THE CONSISTENCY OF OATMEAL (PORRIDGE) (WHICH IS IMPOSSIBLE TO BARBECUE, SO WE'LL IGNORE THAT), OR LEFT TO SET FIRM AND THEN SLICED INTO PIECES BEFORE BEING FRIED OR CHARGRILLED. BINGO! IT'S FANTASTIC JUST SERVED WITH BARBECUED FISH OR MEAT, OR YOU COULD PILE A SLICE OF IT WITH VEGETABLES (I'M THINKING SCALLIONS/SPRING ONIONS, HALVED LITTLE GEM LETTUCES, AND VINE TOMATOES) FLASHED ON THE GRILL, AND SMOTHERED WITH SHAVED PARMESAN AND OLIVE OIL FOR ANY VEGETARIANS WHO CAN'T BE CONVINCED TO TUCK INTO SOME PERFECTLY GOOD MEAT.

2 teaspoons sea salt

7 oz. (200 g) instant polenta/cornmeal, about 1⅓ cups

2 garlic cloves, crushed

1 tablespoon chopped fresh basil

4 tablespoons butter

⅔ cup (50 g) freshly grated Parmesan cheese

freshly ground black pepper

olive oil, for brushing

a rectangular cake pan (tin), 9 x 12 inches (23 x 30 cm), greased

serves 8

★ Pour 1 quart (1 liter) water into a heavy pan and bring to a boil. Add the salt and gradually whisk in the polenta/cornmeal in a steady stream, using a large metal whisk.

★ Cook over low heat, stirring constantly with a wooden spoon, for 5 minutes or until the grains have swelled and thickened.

★ Remove the pan from the heat and immediately beat in the garlic, basil, butter, and Parmesan until the mixture is smooth. Season to taste with black pepper. Pour into the greased cake pan (tin) and let cool completely.

★ Preheat the grill/barbecue. Turn out the polenta onto a board and cut into large squares, then cut in half again to form triangles. Brush the triangles with a little olive oil and cook over hot coals for 2–3 minutes on each side until charred and heated through.

CHAPTER 8

SWEET HEAT

GRILLED FRUIT PACKAGES

I'VE GOT A REALLY SWEET TOOTH, SO THE IDEA OF FOLLOWING A GRILLED MEAT OR FISH (PREFERABLY BOTH) SESSION ON THE BARBECUE WITH SOME FRUIT, ALSO WHACKED ON THE GRILL, IS A SUPERB ONE. THERE'S ABSOLUTELY NO EFFORT INVOLVED IN THIS MIDDLE EASTERN-INSPIRED DESSERT. SHOVEL YOUR FRUIT INTO A FOIL PACKAGE, SLING IT ON THE GRILL, AND WHILE THAT'S DOING ITS THING, PUT SOME YOGURT, HONEY, AND ROSEWATER IN A BOWL TO SERVE WITH THE COOKED FRUIT. IN FACT, IT'S SO RIDICULOUS IN ITS SIMPLICITY THAT I ENCOURAGE YOU TO JOIN ME IN A SMUG LAUGH TO CELEBRATE.

4 peaches or nectarines, halved, pitted, and sliced

8 oz. (225 g) blueberries

4 oz. (125 g) raspberries

freshly squeezed juice of 1 orange

1 teaspoon ground cinnamon

2 tablespoons sugar

1 cup (200 ml) thick plain yogurt

1 tablespoon clear honey

1 tablespoon rosewater

1 tablespoon chopped pistachio nuts, to serve

serves 4

* Put the fruit into a large bowl, add the orange juice, cinnamon, and sugar and mix well. Divide the fruit mixture evenly between 4 sheets of foil. Fold the foil over the fruit and seal the edges to make packages.

* Put the yogurt, honey, and rosewater into a separate bowl and mix well. Set aside until required.

* Preheat the grill/barbecue, then cook the packages over medium–hot coals for 5–6 minutes. Remove from the heat, open carefully, and transfer to 4 serving bowls. Serve with the yogurt and a sprinkling of pistachio nuts.

GRILLED FIGS
with almond mascarpone cream

I'VE MENTIONED IT BEFORE: DON'T BUY NASTY FIGS. GET NICE RIPE ONES, PREFERABLY FROM A GREENGROCER—YOU WON'T REGRET IT. IF YOU'RE READING THIS AND THINKING "DON'T LECTURE ME ON FIGS AGAIN, I DON'T EVEN LIKE THEM, FOOL," THEN THIS RECIPE WORKS PRETTY WELL WITH STONE FRUITS TOO, SUCH AS PLUMS, PEACHES, OR NECTARINES. IF YOU DON'T LIKE ANY OF THAT LOT EITHER, YOU'RE OBVIOUSLY RIDICULOUSLY HARD TO PLEASE AND I DON'T KNOW WHAT TO SUGGEST. PERHAPS SLING SOME GRAPES IN THE MASCARPONE CREAM OR SOMETHING. WHADDYA MEAN YOU DON'T LIKE GRAPES?

★ Put the mascarpone cheese, vanilla extract, almonds, Marsala wine, and honey into a bowl and beat well. Set aside in the refrigerator until required.

★ Put the sugar and ground cardamom into a separate bowl and mix well. Carefully dip the cut surface of the figs into the mixture.

★ Preheat the grill/barbecue, then cook the figs over medium–hot coals for 1–2 minutes on each side, until charred and softened.

★ Transfer the grilled figs to 4 serving bowls and serve with the almond mascarpone cream.

5 oz. (150 g) mascarpone cheese

½ teaspoon vanilla extract

1 tablespoon toasted ground almonds, or slivered almonds crushed to a powder with a mortar and pestle

1 tablespoon Marsala wine

1 tablespoon clear honey

1 tablespoon sugar

1 teaspoon ground cardamom

8–10 figs, halved

serves 4

BANANA PACKAGES

with chocolate and rum

BANANAS ARE LOVELY, PERIOD. BUT I RECKON THEY CAN DEFINITELY BE IMPROVED UPON.
HOW? YOU ASK INNOCENTLY. BY BEING STUFFED WITH CHOCOLATE—THAT'S HOW. BUT IT
DOESN'T STOP THERE, FRIENDS. OH NO. BELIEVE IT OR NOT, THIS
HEAVENLY BANANA/CHOCOLATE COMBO CAN BE MADE EVEN
BETTER. HOW IS THAT EVEN POSSIBLE? YOU ASK, MOUTH AGAPE.
BY DRIZZLING THE WHOLE LOT IN LOVELY RUM. YEAH! SO FAR, SO
AMAZING. BUT THERE'S MORE. IT'S WINTER, AND THE IDEA OF
DRAGGING THE BARBECUE OUT IS MAKING YOU SAD. DON'T
WORRY, DO THEM IN A STOVE-TOP GRILL PAN INSTEAD. THERE IS
NOTHING HOLDING YOU BACK AT ALL WITH THIS RECIPE, IT'S ALL
GOOD. GO MAKE IT.

4 banana leaves or pieces
of foil, cut to 10 inches
(25 cm) square

4 bananas, halved crosswise

4 oz. (125 g) dark chocolate,
broken into small pieces

4 tablespoons dark rum

whipped cream, to serve

kitchen twine or raffia, soaked
in water for 15 minutes
before use

serves 4

★ Put the banana leaves on a work surface. On the first leaf, put 2 banana
halves side by side. Sprinkle with one-quarter of the chocolate and
1 tablespoon rum. Fold up the sides and edges to form a square package.
Tie with the wet twine or raffia (soaking will prevent the twine from
burning). Repeat to make 4 packages.

★ Put the packages on a preheated grill/barbecue and cook for about
10 minutes on each side.

★ Snip the twine and serve with whipped cream.

NOTE Banana leaves are available from Latin-American markets or Asian
stores. To make them more malleable, put on the grill or grill pan for
1 minute before using. Aluminum foil makes a worthy substitute.

BARBECUED PEARS
with spiced honey, walnuts, and blue cheese

IF YOU'RE THE SORT OF INCREDIBLY SOPHISTICATED/PRETENTIOUS HOST WHO LIKES TO END HIS OR HER BARBECUE SESSIONS WITH A CHEESE COURSE, THEN THIS ONE'S FOR YOU. IT'S A BIT OF A CLASSIC AS FAR AS THE FLAVORS GO—PEAR, HONEY, WALNUTS, AND BLUE CHEESE—BUT HERE YOU'RE ADDING SOME LOVELY SMOKINESS BY GRILLING THE PEARS. OF COURSE, IF YOU'RE LESS THAN SOPHISTICATED (LIKE ME) AND YOU'VE MANAGED TO GET TO THE END OF THE BARBECUE STILL STANDING, AFTER DRINKING EVERYTHING YOU COULD LAY YOUR HANDS ON, YOU MAY NO LONGER POSSESS THE FACULTIES TO CHARGRILL YOUR PEARS. DON'T WORRY, USE THEM UNCOOKED, IT'LL STILL BE REALLY NICE.

2 oz. (50 g) walnuts

2 tablespoons clear honey

¼ teaspoon ground cardamom

4 pears

2 tablespoons sugar, for dusting

4 slices of toast

4 oz. (125 g) Gorgonzola cheese

dessert wine, to serve

serves 4

★ Put the walnuts into a skillet or frying pan, add the honey and cardamom, and cook over a high heat until the honey bubbles furiously and starts to darken. Immediately pour the mixture onto a sheet of waxed (greaseproof) paper and let cool.

★ Peel the nuts from the paper and set aside.

★ Preheat the grill/barbecue. Using a sharp knife, cut the pears into quarters and remove and discard the cores. Cut the pear quarters into thick wedges. Dust lightly with sugar and cook over medium–hot coals for about 1½ minutes on each side.

★ Pile the pears onto slices of toast, sprinkle with the walnuts, and crumble over some Gorgonzola cheese. Serve with a glass of dessert wine.

HOMEMADE MARSHMALLOWS

SO, IT'S NIGHT, YOU'RE OUT UNDER THE STARS, SITTING AROUND THE GLOWING EMBERS OF THE CAMPFIRE (OR BARBECUE), AND TOASTING HOMEMADE MARSHMALLOWS ON STICKS WITH YOUR BEAUTIFUL FRIENDS WHILE SHARING SPOOKY STORIES. HOW UNBELIEVABLY CINEMATIC AND COOL DOES THAT SOUND? OF COURSE, IT WON'T BE SO COOL WHEN THE HOOK-HANDED MASKED PSYCHO-SERIAL KILLER SINKS HIS MACHETE INTO YOUR SWEDE AND PICKS YOU ALL OFF ONE BY ONE, LATER IN THE EVENING, BUT THAT PROBABLY WON'T EVEN HAPPEN, SO DON'T WORRY … HONESTLY. MUCH. ANYWAY, MOVING ON, YOU CAN ADD NATURAL FLAVORS OR COATINGS TO YOUR MARSHMALLOWS; CHOCOLATE, STRAWBERRY, AND COCONUT ARE ALL GOOD TO BEGIN WITH. FEEL FREE TO EXPERIMENT, PEOPLE.

3 packages of gelatin—¼ oz. (5 g) each package or ¾ oz. (21 g) total

1 cup (240 ml) cold water

2 cups (200 g) granulated sugar

⅔ cup (200 g) light corn syrup (liquid glucose)

¼ teaspoon salt

2 teaspoons vanilla extract

2 cups (275 g) confectioner's (icing) sugar, for coating the marshmallows

makes 48

★ Put the three packages of gelatin and ½ cup (120 ml) of the cold water in an electric stand mixer. Let rest for about 15 minutes.

★ Combine the sugar, remaining water, corn syrup, and salt in a pan and bring to a boil, stirring constantly. Once a full boil is reached, reduce the heat a pinch, and boil for two minutes. Pour the hot mix into your mixer over the gelatin. Beat on a high speed for 10 minutes—it will become very thick toward the end. Once it's super-thick, add the vanilla and beat for another minute.

★ While the marshmallows are beating, line a 9 x 13 inch (12 x 33 cm) casserole dish with plastic wrap (clingfilm)—sides too. Take some vegetable oil and rub it all over the plastic wrap in the casserole dish—sides too! Now rub the oil on your spatula and a pair of kitchen scissors or a knife. Once the marshmallow is ready, rub the oil on your hands, too.

★ Scrape out the marshmallow into the dish. Use your spatula to get it out and spread it as even as you can in the dish. Let sit for 2–3 hours. It will firm up into one solid piece.

★ After it has set, use your oil-coated knife or scissors to cut strips and then pieces—you can make them large or small. Take each piece and dip all sides in confectioner's (icing) sugar. This will keep them from sticking to each other and anything they come in contact with.

ROCKY ROAD CAMPFIRE S'MORES

with ginger spiced sugar

cookies

1½ cups (200 g) all-purpose (plain) flour

½ teaspoon baking soda (bicarbonate of soda)

½ teaspoon baking powder

½ teaspoon ground ginger

½ teaspoon ground cinnamon

½ teaspoon ground allspice

½ teaspoon ground anise

½ teaspoon ground cloves

a pinch of sea salt

1½ sticks (175 g) unsalted butter, at room temperature

¾ cup (150 g) dark brown sugar

1 egg

1 teaspoon vanilla extract

s'mores

⅓ cup (65 g) cane sugar mixed with 2 tablespoons ground ginger

a large bag of marshmallows

a large bar of plain chocolate

a large bar of milk chocolate

a baking sheet lined with baking parchment

serves 6

IF YOU'RE AMERICAN OR CANADIAN YOU'LL KNOW WHAT A S'MORE IS. IF YOU'RE NOT, YOU'LL PROBABLY BE PONDERING HOW EXACTLY TO PRONOUNCE IT (APPARENTLY LIKE "SNORES") AND WHY YOU SHOULD EVEN CARE. WELL, PREPARE TO GET EDUMACATED! IT'S A TOASTED MARSHMALLOW, SANDWICHED BETWEEN COOKIES (USUALLY GRAHAM CRACKERS/DIGESTIVE BISCUITS), WITH A PIECE OF CHOCOLATE WEDGED IN THERE FOR GOOD MEASURE. HOLY MOLY! THESE SOUND LOVELY, BUT ALSO AS THOUGH THEY'LL FATTEN YOU UP LIKE NOBODY'S BUSINESS. YOU MAY WANT TO ALTERNATE SCOFFING THESE WITH MAD BRISK HIKES AROUND THE GARDEN PERIMETER, WHILE SINGING "THE HAPPY WANDERER."

★ In a mixing bowl, combine the flour, baking soda (bicarbonate of soda), baking powder, ginger, cinnamon, allspice, anise, cloves, and sea salt and set aside.

★ In a separate mixing bowl, cream together the butter and brown sugar with an electric hand mixer until fluffy, then beat in the egg and vanilla extract. Slowly beat in the flour mixture until it forms a dough.

★ Tip the dough onto a sheet of plastic wrap (clingfilm) and roll up into a log. Put in the freezer for 20 minutes.

★ Preheat the oven to 350°F (180°C).

★ Remove the dough from the freezer and slice the log into ¼-inch (½-cm) discs. Arrange the discs on the prepared baking sheet and bake in the preheated oven for 10 minutes. Remove from the oven and sprinkle with the ginger spiced sugar, then return to the oven and bake for a further 5 minutes. Remove from the oven and leave to cool on a wire rack.

★ To make the s'mores, thread marshmallows onto long metal skewers and toast over a fire. Sandwich them between the cookies along with a piece of chocolate, and eat.

MANGO CHEEKS
with spiced palm sugar ice cream

WE'RE NOT TALKING A SLICE HERE, OR EVEN A PIECE, BUT THE "CHEEK" OF A MANGO. I DON'T KNOW ABOUT YOU, BUT THAT SOUNDS PRETTY DARN SEXUAL TO ME. HOLD THAT THOUGHT AND THEN CONSIDER THIS. THE PALM SUGAR ADDS AN INCREDIBLE TOFFEE FLAVOR TO THE ICE CREAM, WHILE THE STAR ANISE OFFERS A HINT OF THE EXOTIC. COMBINE THIS WITH THE WARM MANGO AND, WELL, WHAT CAN I SAY? IF YOU'RE ANYTHING LIKE ME, YOU'RE GETTING BARE-ASS NAKED RIGHT NOW, SAVE FOR YOUR SOCKS (OBVS!), AND PREPARING TO MAKE THIS. DON'T BURN ANY DANGLY BITS ON THE BARBECUE, 'K?

3 large mangoes

confectioner's (icing) sugar, for dusting

spiced palm sugar ice cream

1¾ cups (450 ml) milk

1¼ cups (300 ml) heavy (double) cream

3 oz. (75 g) palm sugar, grated, or soft brown sugar

4 whole star anise

5 egg yolks

serves 4

* To make the ice cream, mix the milk, cream, sugar, and star anise into a heavy pan and heat gently until the mixture just reaches boiling point. Set aside to infuse for 20 minutes. Put the egg yolks into a bowl and beat until pale, then stir in the infused milk. Return to the pan and heat gently, stirring constantly, until the mixture is thickened and coats the back of a spoon. Let cool completely, then strain.

* Put the mixture into an ice cream machine and freeze according to the manufacturer's instructions. Alternatively, pour into a freezerproof container and freeze for 1 hour until just frozen. Beat vigorously to break up the ice crystals and return to the freezer. Repeat several times until frozen. Soften in the refrigerator for 20 minutes before serving.

* Using a sharp knife, cut the cheeks off each mango and put onto a plate. Dust the cut side of each mango cheek with a little confectioner's (icing) sugar.

* Preheat the grill/barbecue, then grill the cheeks for 2 minutes on each side. Cut the cheeks in half lengthwise and serve 3 wedges per person with the ice cream.

TOASTED COCONUT ICE CREAM
with grilled pineapple

GRILLED PINEAPPLE IS ABSOLUTELY SUBLIME, AND IT WORKS BRILLIANTLY WITH COCONUT ICE CREAM, WHICH INCIDENTALLY USES TOASTED SHREDDED (DESICCATED) COCONUT FOR A REALLY NUTTY FLAVOR. IF YOU'RE NOT A FAN OF PINEAPPLE, SUBSTITUTE OTHER FRUITS, SUCH AS MANGOES OR PEACHES, AND IT'LL STILL BE GOOD. IT'S JUST THAT IT WON'T GO SO WELL WITH THE BOTTLE OF MALIBU YOU SHOULD BE NECKING AS YOU COOK. IT'S TRADITIONAL!

½ cup (100 g) brown sugar

1 stick (125 g) unsalted butter

⅓ cup (100 ml) dark rum

1 pineapple, medium or small, with leafy top if possible, cut lengthwise into wedges and core removed

ice cream

⅓ cup (25 g) dried unsweetened shredded (desiccated) coconut

1¾ cups (450 ml) heavy (double) cream

1¼ cups (300 ml) coconut milk

½ cup (100 g) sugar

5 egg yolks

serves 6

★ To make the ice cream, put the coconut in a dry skillet or frying pan and toast, stirring, over medium heat for 2–3 minutes, until evenly browned. Transfer to a pan, then add the cream, coconut milk, and sugar. Heat gently until it just reaches boiling point.

★ Put the egg yolks in a bowl and beat with a wooden spoon until pale. Stir in about 2 tablespoons of the hot custard, then return the mixture to the pan. Heat gently, stirring constantly, until the mixture thickens enough to coat the back of the wooden spoon. Remove the pan from the heat and let cool completely.

★ When cold, strain the custard, and freeze in an ice cream maker according to the manufacturer's instructions. Transfer to the freezer until required. Alternatively, pour the cold custard into a plastic container and freeze for 5 hours, beating at hourly intervals with a balloon whisk.

★ Put the sugar, butter, and rum in a small pan and heat until the sugar dissolves. Brush a little of the mixture over the pineapple wedges, then cook them on a preheated grill/barbecue for 2 minutes on each side until charred and tender. Remove from the heat and, holding the flesh with a fork, cut between the skin and flesh with a sharp knife. Cut the flesh into segments to make it easier to eat, then reassemble the wedges. Serve with the ice cream and remaining rum sauce, about 2 tablespoons each.

INDEX

RECIPE CREDITS

Valerie Aikman-Smith
Smoky chili BBQ sauce
Hogwild bourbon glaze
Hog heaven spice mix
Cherry pomegranate grilled duck skewers
Mint and lemon thyme lamb kebabs with quick pickled cucumber
Porterhouse steak with chimichurri
Grilled skirt steak with smoked butter
Spiced red snapper with chermoula
Grilled vine-leaf-wrapped sardines
Grilled lobsters with two butters
Harissa and pomegranate rack of lamb
Rocky road campfire s'mores

Fiona Beckett
Salsas: Corn and pepper, Salsa verde, and Fresh tomato
Thai lemongrass quail
Chargrilled steak fajitas with chunky guacamole
Tuscan-style steak
Sicilian-spiced seabass

Ghillie Bhasan
Souk kebabs with roasted cumin and paprika
Chicken tandoori kebabs
Chargrilled tamarind shrimp
Pork kofta kebabs with sweet and sour sauce
Spicy beef and coconut kofta kebabs
Lamb kebabs with roasted cumin and hummus
Grilled harissa chicken
Kefta kebabs with harissa couscous
Grilled sardine sandwiches stuffed with chermoula
Lamb and porcini kebabs with sage and Parmesan
Duck satay with grilled pineapple and plum sauce
Vine-wrapped monkfish kebabs
Chargrilled quail with kumquats
Spicy tofu satay with soy dipping sauce
Summer vegetable kebabs with homemade pesto

Vatcharin Bhumichitr
Moo Ping pork

Dr Burnorium:
Simple psycho ribs

Heather Cameron
Homemade marshmallows

Maxine Clarke
Grilled tuna steaks with peperonata
Grilled sardines with salmoriglio sauce
Moroccan butterflied and barbecued lamb
Grilled eggplant with lemon, mint, and balsamic vinegar
Grilled fig and prosciutto bruschetta with arugula

Clare Ferguson
Souvlaki in pita
Paella

Felipe Fuentes Cruz and Ben Fordham
More salsas: Salsa brava, Avocado salsa, Guacamole
Shrimp a la plancha
Grilled corn on the cob

Dan May
Moroccan lamb burgers with pickled cucumber and yogurt dressing
Jerk chicken with lime and caramelized pineapple
Barbecue shrimp marinated in chili and soy

Jane Noraika
Plantain with lime and chili
Eggplant and smoked cheese rolls
Banana packages with chocolate and rum

Elsa Petersen-Schepelern
Barbecue spare ribs with Mexican salsa
Chargrilled shrimp with avocado chile salsa

Louise Pickford
Marinades: Thai spice, Minted yogurt, and Herb, lemon, and garlic
Rubs: Creole, Moroccan, Asian
Sauces: Barbecue sauce, Sweet chili, and Asian barbecue sauce
Bell pepper butter sauce, Piri-piri sauce, and Smoky barbeque sauce
Flavored butters: Caper, Saffron, and Herb
Skewered scallops with coconut dressing
Chicken kebabs Moroccan style
Duck yakitori
Ribeye steak with anchovy butter
Spiced pork burger with satay sauce
Sage-rubbed pork chops
Vietnamese pork balls
Cheeseburger
Tex-Mex burger with chile relish
Hot-smoked creole salmon
Seared swordfish with new potatoes, beans, and olives
Salt-crusted shrimp with tomato, avocado, and olive salad
Barbecued fish bathed in oregano and lemon
Red snapper with parsley salad
Dukkah-crusted tuna with preserved lemon salsa
Clam package with garlic butter
Squid piri-piri
Scallops with lemongrass and butter
Salmon stuffed with herbs
Pepper 'n' spice chicken
Whole chicken roasted on the barbecue
Mexican-style game hen
Tex-Mex pork rack
Chunky eggplant burgers with pesto
Spiced falafel burger
Mushroom burgers with caramelized garlic aïoli
Charred leeks with tarator sauce
Beet and pearl onion brochettes
Roasted bell pepper and asparagus
Grilled rosemary flatbread
Zucchini, feta, and mint salad
Ember-roasted potatoes

Grilled pita salad with olive salsa and mozzarella
Grilled polenta
Vegetable antipasto
Grilled fruit packages
Grilled figs with almond mascarpone cream
Barbecued pears with spiced honey, walnuts, and blue cheese
Mango cheeks with spiced palm sugar ice cream
Coconut ice cream with grilled pineapple

Linda Tubby
Lamb cutlets with salsa salmoretta

Lindy Wildsmith
Sesame sweet potato packets

PHOTO CREDITS

Martin Brigdale
14, 52, 53, 56, 63–64, 72, 78, 101, 105, 109, 110

Heather Cameron
136

Peter Cassidy
16–17, 26, 29, 55, 57–58, 60–62, 67, 69, 80, 81, 83, 94, 107, 117

Richard Jung
27, 31, 34, 36–37, 39, 49, 86, 114

Erin Kunkel
2, 24, 33, 40–44, 71, 74, 76–77, 98–99, 102–103

William Lingwood
111, 122, 134

Ian Wallace
6–8, 10–12, 18, 20, 22, 28, 30, 38, 45, 47–48, 50, 55, 73, 79, 84–85, 87–93, 96, 100, 113, 118–119, 121, 123, 125, 127–128, 131–133, 135, 139–140

Background images © iStock